Like Water in a Dry Land

A JOURNEY INTO MODERN ISRAEL

Bettina Selby

HarperCollins*Publishers*

HarperCollins*Publishers*
77–85 Fulham Palace Road, London W6 8JB

First published in Great Britain
in 1996 by HarperCollins*Publishers*

1   3   5   7   9   10   8   6   4   2

A catalogue record for this book is
available from the British Library

ISBN 0 00 627942 2

Printed and bound in Great Britain by
Caledonian International Book Manufacturing Ltd, Glasgow, G64

This book is for George

Contents

Acknowledgements

Travelling alone, slowly and independently, means that I have to rely on the goodwill of people I encounter along the way. Each journey presents its own particular brand of difficulties and dangers, and that I arrive safely at my destination is, I believe, proof positive that most people have not been uncharitably disposed towards me. Indeed, my travels are invariably marked by countless acts of help and kindness that go far beyond considerations of mere safety. My faith in the basic goodness of ordinary people the world over is confirmed with each journey I make.

This book draws on the experiences of several Middle East travels made over the last ten years, and the number of people to whom I am indebted for acts of generosity has grown so large that I am unable to mention them all. To anyone who comes across this book and remembers the stranger they spoke to and perhaps drank tea with in some village or desert wayside I send them thanks and greetings.

Many people encountered on this journey, particularly in Israel, I cannot thank openly. Amongst those I can name, however, I would particularly like to express my thanks to His Majesty, King Hussein of Jordan, who graciously shared his ideas with me and cemented my resolve for the project. It was also very helpful to be given the opportunity to meet so many of his ministers and advisers in Amman.

A very special thank you is due to the Port Authority of Limassol, and to Captain Bayada in particular, who worked so hard to get me and Roberts aboard a container ship for Beirut when all other routes proved impossible. Also to Captain Vigliaris Ioannis of the Greek ship, Pelrider, from whose bridge deck I caught my first sight of the Holy Land on a bright Christmas morning.

Also to Pascal and François Matta, Sami and all those at the Amchit Camp Ground in Byblos who assisted my first tentative steps in Lebanon. And without the Armenians of Beirut's Bouj Hammoud district, particularly the Torossian family, Silva Karayan and Rita Gurunian and her family, all of whom made me so warmly welcome, I could not have gained so valuable an insight into the daily life of a country in the aftermath of its ruinous civil war.

I enjoyed so much help and hospitality in Amman, that the list would be long indeed, but I feel a special thank you is due to my irrepressibly cheerful driver, Mahmoud, and to the Bedouin women of Jerash who fed me on their roof.

Bill Warnock of World Vision enabled me to see far more of the Gaza Strip than I could otherwise have done and for this I thank him, as well as for his companionship on the bleak journeys there.

The debt I owe to the organizers of Rapprochement Centre and to all the villagers of Beit Sahour, Muslim and Christian, who steadfastly refuse to fall into the trap of hatred no matter what the provocation, is one I feel I share with people of good-will everywhere.

As always I am grateful to the Armenians of Jerusalem whose Quarter remains for me an oasis of sanity. But I also feel deeply indebted to all the citizens of Jerusalem who have endured throughout these difficult years and who have kept the faith in this most holy of cities. To all who helped me understand something of the complexity of the Holy Land today, Jews, Muslims and Christians alike, I offer my warmest thanks.

Finally I would like to thank Clissold and Peggy Teuly who, when my own home had been turned into a demolition site, offered a haven to finish the writing of this book.

Isle of Oxney
January 1996

Author's Note

Because of the uncertain political climate in the Middle East, and in Israel in particular, at the present time, I have disguised the identities of several of the people mentioned in this book. Only those whose public image is well established and whose convictions and opinions are openly expressed have been clearly identified.

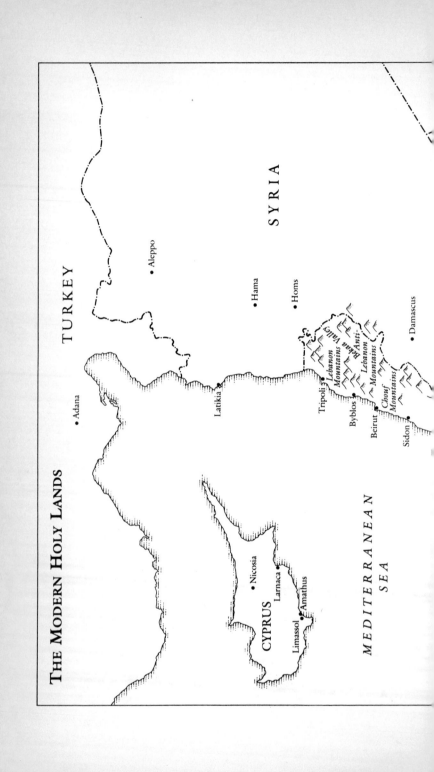

The Modern Holy Lands

TURKEY

SYRIA

• Adana

• Aleppo

• Hama

• Homs

• Damascus

Latikia

Tripoli

Byblos

Beirut

Sidon

Lebanon Mountains

Anti-Lebanon Mountains

Bekaa Valley

Chouf Mountains

MEDITERRANEAN
SEA

CYPRUS

• Nicosia

Larnaca

Amathus

Limassol

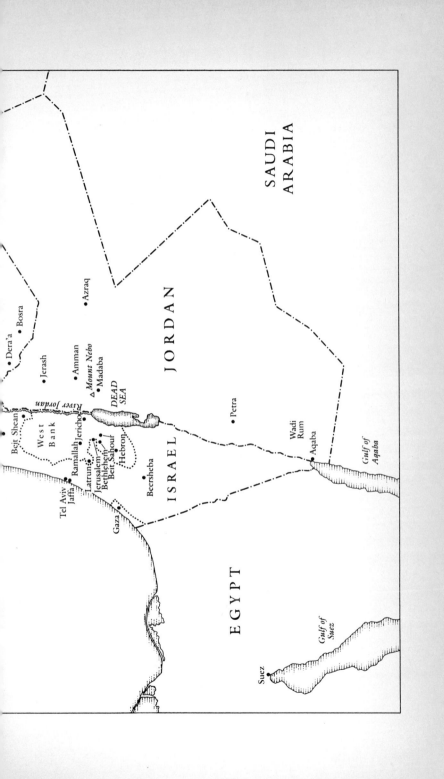

SAUDI
ARABIA

Dera'a • • Bosra

• Azraq

JORDAN

Jerash •   • Amman
                △ *Mount Nebo*
                • Madaba
Beit Shean •

River Jordan

*DEAD
SEA*

West   Jericho•
Bank   • Petra
Ramallah •
Latrun• •Jerusalem   Wadi
Tel Aviv •Bethlehem•   Rum
Jaffa   Beit Sahour•   • Aqaba
            •Hebron•
                                                *Gulf of
            •Beersheba   Aqaba*
Gaza•

ISRAEL

EGYPT

*Gulf of
Suez*

Suez•

Introduction

Jerusalem

The first time I saw Jerusalem was at the end of a long journey. It had taken me five months to get there, travelling by bicycle from England following the routes of the Crusaders and the paths of the early pilgrims. A hard but rewarding journey, it had given me the chance to explore many of the most remarkable sites of the ancient and classical worlds. But even after so rich a feast, arriving at the gates of the Holy City was in no way an anti-climax.

No matter how prepared the traveller might be, the actual stones of Jerusalem come as a shock, as do the signposts with names like 'Mount of Olives', 'Gethsemane', 'Via Dolorosa', 'Holy Sepulchre' . . . Jerusalem has been destroyed and rebuilt countless times in the long span of its history. It is now essentially a medieval city enclosed by the Ottoman walls of Suleiman, but everywhere traces of its many periods break surface, rubbing shoulders with the miscellany of Arab and Crusader buildings.

To touch the fabric of another age gives an insight into the life that was lived there, fleshing it out with a tangible reality, as though for a moment time has compressed and shrunk. This is true even of things as mundane as the ruts scored by chariot wheels in the marble slabs of Roman roads. In Jerusalem, where palpable evidence of past events confronts one on every side, the effect is dramatically heightened because of the nature of what took place there. For people of no particular religious persuasion, as well as for believing Christians, Jews and Muslims, there are moments in Jerusalem when the whole place seems suffused with a sense of the holy.

Herod's vast pavement where the last Temple of the Jews once stood (as for a while did a Roman temple of Jupiter) is now the Haram esh-Sharif – the Noble Sanctuary – and carries the Dome of the Rock, the third most sacred site in Islam. This great golden dome, the most conspicuous landmark in Jerusalem, is built over the summit of Mount Moriah where tradition has Abraham preparing his son for sacrifice. With Abraham and Isaac we have ranged so far beyond the bounds of history that the mind finds it difficult to marry event and place. Even three thousand years is a vast stretch, and that, more or less, is the time that has elapsed since King David captured the place from the Jebusites and made it the capital of Israel.

Standing on this tremendous terrace, overawed by the space and by the weight of all those centuries, the white slopes of the Mount of Olives are only a short stone's throw across the Kidron Valley. Within the huge panorama is almost the entire setting of Christ's Passion. Bethany where Jesus stayed with his friends is just over the hill, the road he would have taken still winds its way across the slope. Most of his triumphal approach to the city with the crowds calling Hosanna and strewing palms before him could have been viewed from this pavement.

The Garden of Gethsemane lies near the floor of the valley, close to the acres of white Jewish graves. Two churches celebrate the site, the exotic cluster of golden onion domes marking the Russian one is slightly higher up the hill than the Franciscan Church of All Nations which is built on the ruins of the original Byzantine basilica.

In the opposite direction, across the jumbled roofs of the city, is the leaded dome of Holy Sepulchre, beneath which lies the site of Golgotha and the closing scenes of the Passion of Christ. The road that links the two, the Via Dolorosa, is somewhere below, twisting its way upwards through the shadowed passages of the city.

But Jerusalem is not just a museum of the past, as I was very soon to discover. It is the home of the first and ongoing church of Christ, founded there from the very beginning. The members of the Palestinian churches who refer to themselves, a little ironically perhaps, as the 'living stones' are the bedrock of Christian life in Jerusalem, their presence the guarantee that the holy sites remain open and accessible to all Christians who wish to come here. Sharing the worship of the Palestinian communities was an important part of being there.

The variety of churches in the city was at first rather bewildering. Eastern and Western, Monophysites and Orthodox – Latins, Copts, Armenians, Jacobites, Maronites, Ethiopians, Greek, Russian (both white and red), Lutheran and even my own Anglican Church – all these, and many I had not yet even heard of, all had their foothold in this the central shrine of Christendom.

The diversity of the worship was also confusing, as were the differing dates for celebrating Easter and other major festivals. These and the territorial claims of the main competing churches within Holy Sepulchre itself come as a shock to many visitors who expect to find unity in this of all places. But from the first I rather enjoyed the jealous guarding of privileges – at least it made a change from the apathy that characterizes so much of modern church life back home. I also found considerable pleasure in the richness and novelty of worship in the various churches. All the many different ways of celebrating the Christian message broadened my own understanding and offered fresh insights.

After that first visit I returned to Jerusalem whenever I could. I made friends in many of the communities, particularly among the Armenians who have their own quarter of the city where I was always sure of a welcome. Given opportunities to attend the major Christian festivals of both the Eastern and Western churches, to meet church leaders, talk with scholars and archaeologists, I was admirably placed for collecting material for a book about the city.

It was a book doomed never to see the light, however, for side by side with my growing understanding of Jerusalem's history and the pleasure I found in her monuments was a growing distress and anger at what was happening there politically. Eventually, the *intifada* began and gathered momentum, and what was already a deeply divided country became ever more tense and violent. No distinction was made by the Israelis between organized terrorism and the actions of ordinary people who were living under an oppressive occupation and finding their situation intolerable.

By this time Israel had been occupying all of the Palestinian territories for more than twenty years. The government had been appropriating land to build Jewish settlements and generally behaving in the high-handed way of all occupying forces throughout history. The *intifada* was really a spontaneous uprising of the young against the ever-worsening conditions; it meant, quite simply, 'we have had enough'.

The stones and the Molotov cocktails thrown by Palestinian youths and children were being answered by the 'iron fist' policy of the Israelis. Hospitals were suddenly filled with children paralysed by plastic bullets, or with arms deliberately broken by Israeli soldiers. As the Palestinian population was subjected to ever increasing pressures, to curfews and to border closures that left them without the means of earning a living; as they watched the accelerated confiscation of land and property, and the general systematic erosion of their liberties, the violence escalated.

I tried to see the situation from both sides, but as most of my friends and the people I had grown to respect were Christian or Muslim Palestinians, it was only to be expected that I should come increasingly to view events from their perspective. Being rooted in a tradition that considers it wrong to take sides or to meddle in other people's politics, I was also increasingly uncomfortable with my own feelings. Repeatedly I attempted to tell myself that it was neither my country nor my struggle; nor were politics my subject. But it was no use. Unable to separate Jerusalem from the atmosphere of injustice and confrontation that filled it, it became in the end too painful to be there, and I gave up all ideas of writing my book.

Before I left Jerusalem on the final visit, Sister Abraham, a most unusual freelance nun and a wise and charismatic friend to many in Jerusalem, gave me a book she had written. It was a history of the Ethiopian religious community, the poorest and possibly the most spiritual of all the religious communities, as well as one of the oldest. On the flyleaf she had written the uncompromising verse from the psalm of exile: 'If I forget thee O Jerusalem, may my right hand lose its cunning . . .'

In the years that followed there seemed little prospect of things getting any better in Israel in the short term. Apart from Egypt's brave and isolated move in recognizing the State of Israel, the news was all bad. The whole Middle East seemed poised on the brink of a disaster that had uneasy parallels with the period of Mongol anarchy that had followed the defeat of the Crusader Kingdom six centuries before. Israel remained open to tourism throughout this period, but not once did I consider returning. I would have been glad to forget Jerusalem altogether if I could, but the belief remained that there was something of great worth still waiting there for me to discover.

The Oslo Peace Accord between Israel and the PLO was unexpected and caught many more people than me by surprise. Jordan following suit with its own separate peace added to the growing belief that the longed for miracle was really taking place. Only at that point could I afford to admit even to myself how much I had missed not only Jerusalem but all of the Holy Land and its people. Had no pressing commitments prevented me, I might well have jumped on an aeroplane there and then.

It was the Autumn of the following year before I was free to consider a Holy Land journey. By that time caution had intervened. After all, what sort of peace did the 'Peace Accord' mean? A temporary halt to the hostilities? A mere cease-fire? Or a real movement towards reconciliation? I did not wish to commit myself to going back only to find the same desperate and unhappy situation.

Jordan, whose politics had been so intimately bound up with those of the Palestinians, and who also held responsibility for the Holy Muslim Places of Jerusalem, might well be the key to the peace of the whole area, I thought. The Jordan/Israel Peace Treaty had only been signed a few weeks before, on 26 October. In an attempt to try and find out what was really happening I wrote to King Hussein and asked if I might possibly have an audience to hear his views on the subject.

A week later I was cordially invited to meet the king at his English home. Half an hour with this courteous and unassuming monarch convinced me at least of the integrity of

Jordan's intentions. King Hussein's belief was in 'a warm peace, a complete peace' and he outlined the many areas in which he looked for co-operation and mutual benefit between his country and Israel. His strongest argument, however, was a moral imperative: 'We have to have peace. What else do we leave behind us for our children and our grandchildren?'

On the question of the Palestinians, however, he could not speak directly. The Palestinians who lived in Jordan were equal citizens, had always been; he could not, he said, have had it any other way. But Jordan had relinquished all responsibility for the West Bank to the PLO. It was now Arafat's responsibility, though he would continue to help him all he could. His hope was that what Arafat symbolized would change, and that he would become a symbol of a people, not of a group. Palestinians had suffered so much in the past six years they would not now accept a dictatorship. They would have to have a right in shaping their future. There would have to be genuine democracy in their choice of government; elections were imperative.

The most obvious necessity for the Palestinians in the West Bank and Gaza, the king said, was a change in their quality of life. There was so much deprivation, hunger, despair, anger; it had got to end somehow. Other countries would have to help. If the mechanism was not there and they received only enough to meet their daily needs, not very much would have been accomplished. There could be no peace without the people having more grounds for hope in a future. But as the king pointed out, the Israeli/PLO Peace Accord was only a declaration of intention, no details had as yet been worked out.

As for the Holy Places, he felt that Almighty God in his wisdom could not have made Jerusalem so important to the three great monotheistic religions had he intended their followers to fight over it. After all, there was a West and an East Jerusalem. West Jerusalem was clearly the capital of Israel whether the rest of the world recognized it or not. East Jerusalem could become the centre of the new Palestinian state. But the Old City of Jerusalem, the walled city with its Holy Places should be outside this equation, since it was the concern of all the followers of the three religions throughout the world.

Introduction

The Holy City should be elevated above any political problems
between Palestine and Israel or the sovereignty of this or that
state. Sovereignty of the Holy Places should be only to the
Almighty.

And as the king was talking so passionately about a Jerusalem
he clearly loved, I remembered suddenly that as a youth of seventeen he had been there in the Haram esh-Sharif, at the
entrance to the El-Aqsa mosque when his grandfather, King
Abdullah, was shot dead at his side by a Palestinian marksman.

It was remembering this incident, more than anything King
Hussein actually said about the peace, that finally decided me to
return there, and to attempt my book again. It is difficult to
explain quite why this was so. It had something to do with real-
izing the efforts of understanding and forgiveness that King
Hussein must have had to make over the incident. But it also
gave me a glimpse of Jerusalem from entirely different eyes,
from the perspective of another religion, and in doing so it
subtly shifted my own outlook on the place. There was a
glimmer of understanding, a brief glance through the shifting
veil. I had a sudden thought that if I went back now – and I
already knew that I would – it would not be a return to familiar
ground, to the city I remembered, but a journey to another
Jerusalem, one I had yet to encounter. And at that point the old
familiar excitement of planning to set out on a new journey
took over.

CHAPTER ONE

Under Way

I set out for Jerusalem half way through December which is not the best time of year for a Holy Land journey, especially not by bicycle. The abundant rainfall of winter in the Middle East had once called a halt to all but the most pressing of overland journeys. Seasoned Crusaders, fearful of rust, had their precious chain mail well wrapped in greasy sheepskins by the beginning of October, and any pilgrim still on the overland route could expect to find the mountain passes blocked by heavy snow.

I could have flown directly there of course. But even had I not wanted to take a fresh look at other parts of the Holy Land on the way I should still have felt the need to approach Jerusalem slowly, and under my own steam. The abrupt departures and arrivals of modern travel do not appeal to me, nor the way that they cause distances to shrink and lose their significance. The whole point of a journey for me lies in the unhurried progress, the opportunities for unexpected meetings, and being able to stop wherever and whenever I choose. A bicycle gives me the sort of freedom and space I need, while demanding sufficient physical effort to be a challenge. And if the fury of the elements or the impossible nature of the terrain makes progress temporarily impossible, both bicycle and rider can usually get a lift on some other means of transport until conditions improve.

Most confirmed travellers are optimists at heart. In the parts of the world I have travelled through I mostly found people well disposed towards a solo traveller, particularly one on a bicycle to whom they can call out a greeting. My vulnerability has served me better than any weapon could have done, but I have also come to believe that I have a guardian angel who looks out for me when danger does threaten or when the going gets really tough. None of this makes me feel justified in skimping the preparations for a journey or in not employing adequate precautions, but it does make me prepared to take what I think of as reasonable risks.

Even an optimist would not willingly choose to take a laden cycle through snow, sleet and flood, but further researches into the likely winter weather patterns of the Holy Land were not entirely doom and gloom. 'Greater Syria is an area of wide climatic variation,' claimed one source, 'and subject to sudden dramatic changes. Winter storms can give way abruptly to settled days of warm sunshine.' Pinning my hopes on a dramatic change in the current spate of rain, snow and blizzards, I decided that there was no real reason not to bicycle to Jerusalem.

There was not the time to cycle all the way from London, however, as I had done on my first unforgettable Jerusalem journey, so as an alternative starting point I decided on Cyprus. The island's connection with the Holy Land which goes back to the earliest days of Christianity made it a natural choice, while its position in the north-eastern corner of the Mediterranean offers a convenient stepping stone from or to any port on the Holy Land coast.

Cyprus was the point of departure for St Paul's first great missionary journey when, accompanied by St Barnabas, and a young man who was possibly St Mark, he crossed over to the island from Antioch on his way to Asia Minor. It was the brief account of Paul's visit to Cyprus in Acts that first made me aware of the excellent conditions for independent travel that existed in the Roman Empire of his day, a feature that undoubtedly contributed to the rapid spread of Christianity. Roman peace coupled with splendid Roman roads; the wealth of shipping carrying Roman trade to the far corners of the Empire, and with Greek as the lingua franca, the whole of the classical Mediterranean world could be traversed with an ease that today's traveller faced with problematic borders on every hand, kidnapping and no-go areas might well envy. I anticipated no particular problems on this journey, however. How wrong that expectation was to prove, I would discover soon enough.

One of the numerous cheap flights from London to Cyprus landed me in Larnaca airport at three in the morning, an hour that would have been decidedly more irksome had I not been able to make use of some of the unsociable time by re-assembling my bicycle. Most airlines insist that bicycles in transit have their pedals removed and the handlebars turned round sideways to take up less space. The tyres also have to be deflated because it is believed that if this is not done they will explode in the unpressurized luggage hold. This is in fact a complete fallacy, but one so firmly fixed in air travel mythology that there is no point in arguing about it; better to save one's breath for pumping up the tyres again at the far end.

In addition to the preparations required by the airline, I also wrap my bicycle in foam pipe lagging to cushion the tubing and the vulnerable working parts. A cardboard sleeve is then tied over it to hold it all in place and, when flying British Airways, an enormous plastic bag is supplied which engulfs the entire machine. I have had cycles badly damaged in flight, in spite of such precautions, and the worry that I will arrive at the start of a long journey with a totally unrideable machine prevents me relaxing until I have unwrapped it at the far end and assured myself that all is well.

On this occasion, the bicycle had not been inadvertently left behind, nor had playful baggage handlers taken turns to see how far they could toss it across the tarmac. Nor had anyone piled heavy crates on top of it and buckled the wheels. It had not even been forced through the narrow opening onto the luggage carousel shedding bits and pieces of itself as it went (all fates suffered by bicycles of mine on previous flights).

This journey started well. An hour and a half after landing, with all bandaging removed, handlebars realigned, pedals replaced, tyres inflated, brakes and gears adjusted, my red Roberts bicycle – lively veteran of a tricky journey through the mountains of Kurdistan – was once more fit and ready for the road. Hooking on the four panniers which contained my entire needs for the next few months, I sallied forth under a star-filled Mediterranean night.

At this cold hour before dawn my breath hung like a cloud in the air before me, but since the temperature in Cyprus was several degrees higher than the arctic conditions prevailing in London I had an illusion of warmth. After the work of getting the cycle ready in the overheated airport lounge the bracing chill was welcome, especially when coupled to Mediterranean scents, the murmur of waves and this brighter than remembered sky. It was with a sense of exhilaration that I set off eastward with the sea on my right hand.

As my blood warmed to the exercise and the pedals started to spin I also awoke to the full realization that at last I was really on my way. The adventure was afoot. All the planning and the decisions, the scurrying around over last minute hitches and difficulties were now behind me and no new problems had as yet presented themselves. This all too brief period that comes at the start of every journey is exquisite. Life seems suddenly entirely carefree and full of a heady freedom. The way ahead promises only pleasant prospects. I savoured the moment joyfully.

Above the faint swishing of tyres on a gritty road came the sound of small waves slapping at the jetties and running hissing over the pebbles. Otherwise the silence was profound; not even a seabird called. A wavering line of white foam edged the blackness of the sea from which the lovely Aphrodite had emerged. The oracle of Aphrodite of Paphos was in reality a shapeless volcanic stone, housed now in the museum of Nicosia. It has, it seems, nothing at all in common with Botticelli's luminous painting of the beautiful young daughter of Neptune riding ashore on a scallop shell. An eastern goddess, the archetypal Aphrodite represented the dark and primitive forces of fecundity and death, very close to the great Earth Mother. It must have been after her gradual metamorphosis into a shapely and desirable female form representing the more erotic aspects of procreation that she gave Cyprus the reputation of being the Island of Love.

Thinking about Aphrodite, or Venus as the Romans knew her, and wondering whether the bright planet hanging low in the southern sky was the one named for her, I soon found myself riding into Larnaca's empty, lighted streets. The sea was still murmuring on my right, but further off now and fainter as

pavements and esplanades intervened. Without its close presence my energies suddenly slumped. Sleeping houses and shuttered hotels now surrounded me, making me feel shut out and
very tired. Since it was inconceivable that there would be any
sort of hotel or guest house open at this hour, I thought the
best I could do would be to find a corner to huddle down in my
sleeping-bag till daylight. I carry the basic necessities of self-suf-
ficiency for just such occasions, but I couldn't seem to find anywhere private enough in this little seaside town, nor could I
raise the energy to ride out again into the countryside.

While in this state of indecision I caught sight of a church
spire, and as churches often have some sort of sheltered porch I
rode off towards it, and in doing so stumbled upon the town's
Youth Hostel. The familiar YH signpost directed me through
an archway whose battered elegance of line suggested Crusader
work. It might have been the entrance to a fortified camp, but
whatever had once stood within had long since been demolished and I found myself in a large cleared space bordered with
what in the dim lighting looked like roughly built garages and
sheds. Against one wall, besides other scraps of Crusader
masonry a long flight of rickety wooden steps led up to an
equally rickety wooden verandah fronting dilapidated-looking
rooms. A handwritten placard in a window announced that the
door was open and that everyone was welcome. The first claim
at least was true. The door opened onto a littered greasy
kitchen full of unwashed crockery and battered pans bearing
the remains of food. Beyond was a hallway, off which were several rooms. The one with a female symbol on the door was
undoubtedly tacky, though less so than the kitchen. It contained about twelve bunk beds, all of them empty of bodies,
and in my exhausted state it looked welcoming enough.

Somehow I found the necessary energy to haul bicycle and
luggage separately up the long steep stairway. Locking Roberts
to the railings I carried the panniers inside. It was the work of a
moment to locate my sleeping-bag, and although it bothered
me a little that there was no lock to the door of the room, I
placed a chair in front of it, so I would hear if it was opened,
and took my few valuables into the sleeping-bag with me. I

could do no more, and with a sense of duty accomplished I had the rare experience of feeling myself drop into unconsciousness.

Voices awoke me talking outside the thin partition of the room. Glancing at my watch I saw I had been asleep for just an hour and a half. Bright sunlight transformed the shabby room, and as there seemed little chance of getting any more sleep I dressed and went out to see what the day held.

The first shock was the discovery that the boat I was proposing to take to the Lebanon was no longer running. Steve, the hostel owner, self-professed 'entrepreneur with a few lines on the side, like this hostel', said the ship had broken down and would not be operational again until June. The golden light dancing on the steel-blue sea suddenly looked less lovely. I gulped down the proffered cup of tea, trying to ignore the stains on the grimy cup, and set off to make further enquiries at the port.

Larnaca is to the south of the antique port of Salamis where St Paul made his landfall. A major port of the classical world until it was destroyed in a massive earthquake, Salamis would have been a far greater loss to shipping than Larnaca could ever be. Why so many shipping agents even bothered to open their office when there was so little business, I could not imagine. I spent a frustrating morning visiting them all, as well as the premises of the numerous travel agents. Over a very late lunch I took stock of the information I had gleaned.

It was scant enough. Every one had confirmed that there were no passenger boats out of Larnaca. The only regular way at present to get from Cyprus to Lebanon was by air, and even that was impossible for the next few weeks, as all flights were fully booked over the Christmas season. Even had I been able to book a flight, the only two airlines that operated the route were not recommended as bicycle transporters.

There were rumours of a few rare luxury liners cruising around the North African shores, and calling at Cypriot and Levantine ports en route. These went from Limassol rather than Larnaca and I had just missed one. There would not be another for a few weeks.

This left only cargo vessels, St Paul's *modus vivendi* and ideal for a bicycle traveller. But whereas cargo ships had once welcomed the additional income from a passenger or two, with the more stringent port and safety regulations and the vagaries of immigration control, the sideline of ferrying passengers is no longer worth the hassle. If a cargo ship could be found to take me the short distance to the Levantine shore it would be as a favour and very difficult to arrange. It was a depressing morning's work, and although some of the agents made vague promises about what might show up on the morrow, no one held out any real hope.

Sitting on a bench beside the sea, waiting for the sunset, I fell into a day-dream about an amphibious bicycle that would give me the freedom of the sea as well as the land. But so tired was I that I fell well and truly asleep with my head slumped on my chest and awoke a good hour later to find that I had missed the sunset. Only a faint afterglow remained and the air had turned decidedly chilly. A full night's sleep was clearly indicated before making any further efforts to leave the island, so I bought some food to cook and cycled back to the hostel.

There were three other guests, all male. I had briefly made their acquaintance early that morning when all three had jerked upright in their beds after I had mistaken the symbols on the dormitory doors and entered the wrong one. I now discovered that the man who had let fly with what I had assumed was a string of Icelandic oaths was in fact a Norwegian called Sten, a painfully thin man, around sixty I thought, but dressed in tight denim jeans and sporting a wealth of tattoos and friendship bracelets. It did not take long to discover that Sten, maudlin and aggressive by turn, had a particularly bad drink problem.

Hubert, a slightly-built, young Austrian carpenter provided Sten with a focus for his bursts of aggression. There was something about Hubert's accent that made Sten think he was being mocked. The other hosteller, a thickset Japanese man of indeterminate age appeared to regard the whole company with an air of inscrutable contempt.

We sat together in close proximity so as to make the most of a pathetically inadequate oil stove. The day had been warm enough to cycle without a jacket but once the sun was down the temperature had plummeted. Cold air was pouring in through gaps in every wall of the ramshackle building. As is the custom for travellers and pilgrims the world over when they meet in such places, we three Occidentals told each other something of our lives and circumstances. The Japanese man followed our exchanges with unsmiling concentration, but contributed nothing.

Sten's story was the all too familiar alcoholic's experience of the slow break-up of his life. He had been a sailor, but had lost job, wife, children, and even, he confessed, his memory, as drink clouded more and more of his mind. He had come to Cyprus for the cheap booze, and also in the hope that someone would take pity on him over Christmas, a time, he said, when he most felt the loss of his family. In the meantime Steve, the hostel owner, was providing him with a free bed and food in exchange for helping out with the cleaning.

Hubert, like me was in transit, kicking his heels in Larnaca while he waited for a cancellation on a flight to Damascus. He too was something of a Christmas waif, but in his case he was escaping from his family. The youngest of seven children, the marriage of his parents and those of his siblings had done nothing to persuade him that he wanted a similar life style. Family Christmases he found so difficult and unpleasant, he said, that he always arranged his annual holidays so as to be away for them. This year he had decided at the last moment to make a lightning tour of the Middle East. He was at the top of the airline's waiting list, and thought there was a good chance he would get off in the next day or two. An easygoing young man, he shrugged off Sten's vicious remarks, which, as the evening progressed and the level in the raki bottle sank, became increasingly aggressive.

Sten needed to be the centre of attention, and when Hubert or I addressed a remark to each other he suspected he was being slighted or that a plot was being hatched against him. His attacks were always followed, after a pause, by offers all round of his raki bottle. Only the silent Japanese man ever accepted.

We tried to draw the Japanese man into the conversation, but apart from telling us his name was Momaro, he was tight as a clam. His answer to any direct question, such as 'What is your work?' would elicit only an 'I would rather not say', in the sort of voice that made his listeners suspect some dark and shameful employment. This, coupled with his close observation of us all was somewhat unnerving. I soon gave up and went to bed.

Next morning Sten was in an evil mood, clumping about with a bucket and mop, while the rest of us tried to get ourselves something to eat in the chaotic kitchen. He seemed determined to earn his keep with the maximum amount of noise and disruption. The water was slopped around with abandon but without achieving any noticeable effect on the mess and grime. I abandoned attempts at breakfast and went to follow up yesterday's leads for my passage to Lebanon.

With no more luck than on the previous day, the best advice seemed to be to pull out of Larnaca and try the port of Limassol, forty miles along the coast. Whatever the outcome, I would not have been prepared to spend another night in the tacky hostel with the tiring, unpredictable moods of Sten. My panniers were already packed. I paid a brief visit to the town's small market for bread, olives, cheese and fruit and headed west.

It was the opposite direction to which I wished to go, but even so it was a joy to be under clear blue skies in bright sunshine. With the rare blessing of a tail wind, I bowled effortlessly over the gentle Cypriot hills. A newly-built modern highway carried what traffic there was, leaving the old road entirely free. It all added up to cycling so perfect that I was able to forget my ongoing transport worries for a while.

The one event of the day was coming upon the splendid ruins of an ancient Greek city. I hadn't noticed the site marked on my small-scale map so it was a complete surprise, and its appearance could not have been better timed. With an abruptness that shocked, I had come to the end of my pastoral idyll and entered upon the last ten-mile stretch into Limassol. Along that entire distance there stretched an unbroken line of new holiday hotel complexes, so brash and new that they looked as though they had sprung up there overnight, like dragons' teeth, with hardly space enough for a glimpse of the sea between them.

I had hardly adjusted to the shock of this sudden intrusion of the late twentieth century or to bemoan not stopping earlier for my picnic when in unlikely and extraordinary contrast, the ruins of Amathus appeared on the landward side of the road.

Eating bread and olives beside a Greek agora, which even in ruins retained the form and genius of its age, had me thinking of St Paul for the first time since landing. He must have passed here on his way to Paphos. Proud as he was of Tarsus, his own 'no mean city', he would surely have approved of Amathus with its expansive public buildings, theatres, fountains, baths. Had he already realized how open the Greeks were to new ideas? Perhaps even here in this very agora he began his ministry. I could well imagine a group of two or three Greeks strolling over to exchange a few words with the strangers who, perhaps like me, had stopped to refresh themselves. And having spoken with them, calling out to friends to come and hear what this remarkable Jew had to say.

It could well be that it was on Cyprus that Paul came to the realization of what his great role was to be. Up to that point the disciples had preached the gospel message only to Jews. Since the Diaspora, some 600 years earlier, Jews were widely scattered all over the known world, and where there were Jews there were synagogues. It was the custom in these synagogues for discussions of a religious nature to take place after the prayers and the scriptural readings, which was the opportunity for the disciples to give their sermons. This is why the three were on Cyprus: '. . . from thence they sailed to Cyprus. And when they landed at Salamis they preached the word of God in the synagogues of the Jews' (Acts 13:4–5).

At this time there was no idea of Christianity as a separate religion, even the word 'Christianity' had not yet been coined. The disciples preached the death and resurrection of Jesus of Nazareth as a part of the Jewish religion. Jesus was the fulfilment of Jewish scripture, the Messiah foretold by the prophets, with his roots deep in the fabric of Jewish history.

The Jewish religion was an essential part of their national identity, and as the 'chosen people' it was exclusive to Jews.

There was no tradition of Jews attempting to convert others to their beliefs. By bringing the gospel of Jesus directly to the Gentile world and with it, the whole corpus of Jewish religious belief – the Law and the Prophets – Paul was making a profound break with Jewish tradition. Whether he took the conscious decision to do this, to become the Apostle to the Gentiles, during the time he was in Cyprus is not known for certain. We do know he was sent for by the governor at Paphos, and that he was able to get the better of the governor's 'false prophet' during the audience. It could be that it was at this point that the decisive experience befell Paul for when, a short time later, Acts has the disciples leaving the island for Asia Minor, Paul is no longer said to be accompanying Barnabas, but is in charge of the party. Also from that time forward he is never again referred to by his Jewish name of Saul. With the adoption of the Roman version, Paul, he might well have been publicly proclaiming the universal nature of his mission.

I spent so much time exploring the ruins of Amathus and thinking about St Paul that in spite of my helpful tail wind, I arrived in Limassol only as the port was closing for the night. Fortunately the Tourist Office was open and a cheerful young woman there was able to direct me to what accommodation was available just three days before Christmas. In the middle of a street of rather bleak warehouses I found myself installed in the Aphrodite Guest House, an unlikely haven at the top of a long flight of stone steps awash with pots of rampant greenery. More abundant greenery overflowed from pots and containers within, sharing the crowded space with a couple of small working fountains, several cages crammed with flocks of twittering birds, and a wealth of assorted kitsch. The walls too were closely hung with bright nick-nacks and large prints of such subjects as the small weeping boy and the green oriental woman, which turn up all around the world.

Quite out of keeping with this cosy and womb-like interior was the decidedly glacial temperature. In Mediterranean countries where only a few months of the year are likely to be cold, many houses are entirely without heating. Even high in the mountains where night temperatures are close to freezing people often seem prepared to shiver until Spring. The elderly strawberry-blonde lady who presided over the Aphrodite was the privileged owner of a small glassed-in cubicle with an electric fire and a television set. From here she could watch the comings and goings of her guests in comfort, and understandably she wasted no time in returning there, having first informed me that I would probably need the blankets from both the beds in my room.

I used up some of the chilly evening hours to make another fruitless round of travel agents who, like the shops, stay open until late. A meal of local fish and a bottle of the excellent light island wine offered some relief before I retired to bed, the only warm place to read and write my journal.

In spite of my growing worries about getting off the island sleep came quickly. As usual at the start of a journey I found I was not as fit as I might be, and the forty-mile ride and fruitless tour of travel agents had rather taken it out of me. Once or twice in the small hours I surfaced to the familiar tugs of anxiety but was mercifully able to sink back into sleep before they could awaken me fully.

Chapter Two

Hopes Raised, Dashed, and Raised Again

Morning, as always, brought a renewed sense of hope and purpose. After boiling water on my stove for a cup of coffee I set out for the port with the fully-laden Roberts. I had settled my account with the Aphrodite but caution made me warn the landlady that I might well be returning for a further night.

Once I had managed to get past the gatekeeper, who was suspicious of cyclists, the port authority turned out to be a model of efficiency and helpfulness. After explaining my problem to the sympathetic harbour master, he passed me on to his senior pilot, Captain Bayada.

To this immensely reassuring man who had spent a good part of his life criss-crossing the oceans of the world, the short hop across to the Levantine shore was no more than the most minor of obstacles. A ship could certainly be found for me, the only difficulty was when, for until his daily mid-morning briefing session with the shipping agents he had no idea of what vessels were sailing, or where to. As there was no way of knowing shipping movements in advance, it would be a matter of my coming to the port each day until the right ship was found. There was still an hour before this day's briefing, and as he had no other ships to pilot in or out, he invited me to take coffee with him, and we sat sharing reminiscences of countries we had both visited, a subject that could have been happily pursued far beyond the time at our disposal.

While Captain Bayada was at the briefing I was given the run of his office, the walls of which were covered with charts and posters. Most of these explained the procedures involved in the piloting of vessels. Every movement, including the boarding and the leaving of ships, and what kind of ladders and ropes were permitted, and which were forbidden, was set out precisely. There was also a splendid machine that kept printing out details of the prevailing weather conditions in the various sectors of the Mediterranean, including wind speeds and directions, a subject that interests cyclists quite as much as sailors.

Nor I discovered had that romance of the sea been entirely destroyed by modern travel. A chart intended to describe the appearance of the sea in different wind forces was couched in language as evocative as poetry. 'Glassy seas', 'a fishing smack begins to heel over', 'ships invisible between the troughs of mountainous waves', and 'the air full of flying foam' plunged me straight into the heroic days before container ships and oil tankers had made their appearance. So complete a picture of a pilot's life could be gained from all these charts that although I was left kicking my heels for an hour and a half, I hardly noticed the time passing.

I was in luck, announced Captain Bayada, coming in suddenly, as I was still mulling over the effect of those towering seas and storm force winds. There was a ship sailing late that afternoon for Tartous in Syria, and as long as my visa was in order I could sail in her. I had not planned on Tartous which was north of Lebanon, but looking at it on one of the charts I could see no reason why not; it was a very good place to begin my ride south.

There was just one snag: I had no Syrian visa. I had not been planning to go through Syria this time unless I had no choice. My plan was to ride down through Lebanon which I had never seen, and enter Israel from the north. Only if that border proved impossible would I have to go back to Beirut, and cross the Lebanon and the Anti-Lebanon Mountains to approach Israel via Syria and Jordan.

Nonetheless, because any border with Israel can prove problematical, I had intended to be prepared for all eventualities and to obtain any visa that might prove useful before leaving London. Both the Jordanian and the Lebanese Consulates had issued me with visas on the spot, but Syria, which adopts a more suspicious attitude towards travellers, particularly writers, required several weeks to 'consider my case'. A hurriedly planned journey was no excuse to cut corners as far as they were concerned. If I did decide to go through Syria, one official at their consulate told me, I could probably get a short-term visa at the Lebanese border. What at the time had seemed just one of the minor irritations of long-distance travel, now loomed large.

I had also been told in London that there was no point in trying to get a Syrian visa in Cyprus as they were issued only to British subjects resident there. My previous experiences with Syrian officialdom did not dispose me towards optimism, but as Captain Bayada remarked, it was worth trying. A telephone call to the Syrian Ambassador elicited an unexpectedly affable response: Yes, certainly, he would help all he could. If the British Embassy would supply an appropriate letter, and if I got it to him by two-thirty that afternoon, I could have my visa.

My phone call to the British Embassy received an equally unexpected response; it was unfriendly almost to the point of hostility. Such sentiments as: 'Well I suppose you can prove you are British', and 'I hope you do not intend to make trouble for us over there' did not seem remotely appropriate to the circumstances. Nonetheless, the official responsible for these and similar churlish remarks did promise to produce the necessary letter, claiming he knew exactly what was required. He would not fax it to the Syrians to save precious time, however, as before receiving it, I must hand over the equivalent of five pounds sterling, and he seemed unable to trust me to do this by post.

Captain Bayada was in the meantime arranging for a taxi. I would have to go to Nicosia, the capital, where all the foreign embassies are to be found. As Nicosia is over forty miles from Limassol it would be a close call if I was to beat the clock, especially as the normal traffic jams of Nicosia would be exacerbated by Christmas holiday traffic.

And so it proved. The driver entered into the spirit of the occasion and tore along the highway like a maniac. Finding the way to the British Embassy through the no man's land that divides the town into Greek and Turkish parts was even more nightmarish. The driver was not familiar with the streets and the one-way systems. He was frightened, he said, of being shot by the trigger-happy Turks if he went the wrong way. I was far more frightened of his driving. And all of it was to no avail. When we finally located the Syrian Embassy and I handed over my letter and passport the buoyed-up hopes froze on the instant and shivered into a thousand pieces.

It was only two days before Christmas so I shall charitably assume that the choleric official at the British Embassy who had penned the one-line letter at such inflated cost had been celebrating prematurely, for even the Syrians laughed at it. In the middle of accusing me of being a spy the Ambassador, flanked by two or three strong hatchet-faced aides, waved the epistle in my face. 'You see?' he said, 'Your embassy does not even use the word "help" only saying you are Mrs Bettina Selby, holder of British passport. I am seeing this for myself in passport. This is not diplomatic letter. I think you were refused visa in London; why else you have Lebanese and Jordan visas and not Syrian? I think we keep your passport. Wait downstairs.'

The effect of the headlong progress had left no time for me to realize how hungry and thirsty I was, having had neither breakfast nor lunch. The day by now was as hot and sticky as the night had been cold, and I longed for a drink. Nonetheless, there was nothing I could do but wait patiently and hope that I would be given another opportunity to persuade the Syrian Ambassador and his suspicious henchmen of my good and honest intentions.

They played an elaborate cat and mouse game with me for an hour, calling me back in for further questioning, waving my passport around in the air as though it was something not quite nice, and telling me to 'Go and wait while we talk about your case.' I was not sure that they would even return my passport, let alone grant me a visa for Syria. In the unlikely event of them coming up trumps and giving me both passport and visa, I reckoned the ship would have sailed by the time I got back to Limassol. And all the while the meter on my taxi was ticking away outside.

I thought of all the splendid Crusader buildings I could have been visiting instead of kicking my heels in that dusty, airless room. For this sad divided city of Nicosia was once the proud capital of a Crusader island.

Richard Cœur de Lion captured Cyprus in the twelfth century, while on his way to join the Third Crusade. At the time he was suffering one of his frequent cash crises and was forced almost immediately to sell the island to the Knights Templar. The Templars did not keep it long either, for soon afterwards the Crusader Kingdom of Jerusalem fell to Saladin who set about clearing the entire Holy Land of Western knights and their families. Guy de Lusignan, King of Jerusalem, bought Cyprus from the Templars to be the base for the reconquest of his kingdom, a dream he shared with at least half of Western Christendom.

For the next three hundred years, until the Ottoman Turks captured Cyprus in the sixteenth century, the wealth of the Lusignans was expended in beautifying the island with fine walled towns, Crusader churches, castles and fortifications. It was their way of filling in time before their eventual return to the Holy Land, for the Lusignans never relinquished their hope, and crowned each new heir with the proud and empty title, King of Jerusalem.

There was never to be a return. The fortunes of the house of Lusignan – Kings of Jerusalem, Armenia and Cyprus – had been decided long ago, in AD 1187, when Saladin brought the short lived Christian kingdom to its end at the Battle of the Horns of Hattin. But for centuries the Lusignan line was maintained and the descendants intermarried with many of the royal houses of Europe. The official end to the dream came only in the nineteenth century when the last of the proud line, an unmarried governess, Eliza de Lusignan, died in obscurity in a London suburb.

The great cathedral where the Lusignan crownings had taken place, and all of the other fine Crusader churches, many of them turned into mosques by the Ottomans and all full of interest and beauty, would have to wait until I returned, for eventually my patience and diplomacy were rewarded. My passport was handed back to me duly stamped with a Syrian visa, and everyone now smiled and shook my hand and hoped that I would enjoy my stay in Syria. Actually it might not have been diplomacy that won the day after all, because the one month visa cost me the best part of forty pounds, and at that price the Syrians might well have considered it worth the risk of letting in a possible spy.

By flouting the island's speed limit once again the taxi got me to the port by ten to four. The Jad was due to sail at four. Kind Captain Bayada had gone home but he had left word with a colleague to see me on to the boat. We collected my bicycle and after clearing immigration, arrived all in a flurry at the side of a scrubby looking vessel. A tiny dark-skinned man in a dirty white jersey and stained jeans peered suspiciously at us from the top of the gangplank. Yes, he was the captain, but no, he could not take me to Tartous, no matter what the agent had promised. It was more than life was worth. The Syrians would question him for days, they would pull his ears off, torture his crew. And after all that they would not allow me to land. They would make him take me back where he had found me. We did not know what the Syrians were like. He did, and it would be worse for him because he was in fact Lebanese.

What could I say? I had experienced considerable hassle with Syrian border posts myself in the past (though never had my ears been pulled). Ports were probably far worse. I could not wish any man to be badly treated on account of helping me across this irritatingly impassable stretch of water. I wished him a pleasant voyage and turned away to hide my disappointment. Ninety pounds the day had cost me so far, and I had left my hat and gloves in the taxi. I was dehydrated, hungry and very, very tired. What was worse, I was no nearer the Holy Land. Defeated I crept back to the verdant but cold Aphrodite.

Christmas Eve dawned with the same bright and flawless skies as I cycled the now familiar path to the port. Captain Bayada, surprised to see me still in Cyprus held out little hope of a departure on this last day before Christmas. The Seaman's Mission of which he was a good friend might be an interesting place to spend the day? Perhaps I could even be of use with the distribution of the traditional Christmas gifts to the seamen in port. Kind thoughts indeed, and I certainly needed something to take my mind off my own concerns for a while.

From the little haven above the immigration offices, the strains of Christmas carols blared forth cheerfully from a hi fi. I had been introduced to a jolly bunch of British ex-pats and was helping to count out gift-wrapped packages into plastic bags. Sailors of various nationalities drifted in, shook hands, and everyone wished everyone else a Happy Christmas. I was deeply into the season of goodwill, glass in hand when Captain Bayada came in from the briefing. He too was all smiles and very happy to tell me I would be sailing later that day aboard a Greek container ship bound for the port of Beirut. Nothing at all, he added, was going to be allowed to go wrong with this arrangement.

After this news the day seemed pure celebration. As more ex-pats and their spouses gathered, and the mince pies and Christmas cake went their rounds, and glasses were recharged, Bethlehem and the birth of the Christ Child seemed suddenly very close. What I had been thinking about St Paul only a couple of days before, and which had been pushed from my mind by all the rushing around and the general worries of travel, now came pressing back. Here we all were celebrating that same Good News that Paul had brought to a wider world, news that was at the heart of this journey. Soon I would be on my way again towards the place where it had all begun.

Feeling a need to be absolutely sure that no last minute hitch was going to spoil the plans, I joined the Greek ship, Pelrider, hours before it was ready to sail. I also wanted to be by myself for a little to think about the way ahead, and decided that any more of the thick brown Cyprus sherry in the Seaman's Mission was likely to cloud the adventure.

With the friendly send off still ringing in my ears, I cycled across the quays, dodging the mammoth cranes and the stacks of containers trundling down the rails. I checked the name on the prow of the vessel at the quay indicated – Pelrider of Piraeus, my ship! Almost before I had time to savour the moment I was following a cheerful young sailor striding up the bobbing, swaying gangplank with Roberts on his shoulder, while another followed behind with the panniers dangling from his fingertips as though they weighed no more than paper bags.

I was clearly expected though no one actually said anything, just smiled and gestured for me to follow. Roberts was tied to a rail and the young man with my luggage led me up several flights of stairs. I was installed just under the bridge deck in a spare cabin next to the captain's. It had clearly been used as a store and hurriedly prepared for me, as the brand new bar of soap and roll of lavatory paper placed upon my table showed. It was a cheerful little cabin with a washroom attached, and also appeared to possess a heating system, a real joy after the frigid Aphrodite.

The bunk was roomy, furnished with a clean sheet and a blanket, and there was a bedside lamp to read by. One of the three opening portholes was so placed that I would be able to see the sky while lying down. There was also a sizeable table to work at. The only problems were that the electricity seemed not to be functioning, and the water in the washroom would not flow. After a little investigation with my useful seven-bladed penknife, however, both these services were restored. With everything now in a workmanlike state I felt I could have spent many happy days in this cabin, instead of the single night the voyage would take.

Down several decks in the wardroom where strong black coffee was constantly on the go and served up in half-pint mugs, a Christmas tree with coloured blinking lights was the one concession to the season. Half the twenty-two members of the crew were half Greek and half Asiatic and, one of them informed me, all were friends. There certainly seemed to be a cheerful egalitarian atmosphere in the ship, with captain, mate and seamen sharing the same wardroom. Several of the men came and introduced themselves or just sat and smiled as if they were too shy to talk or did not know English – all of which made me feel I was a not unwelcome diversion. The Pelrider, I learnt from the chief engineer, a Syrian, plied a fixed route around the Mediterranean, stopping at the same ports on a three-week rota which gave the men very little time to spend with their families.

All the while, without pause the loading continued. The huge cranes plied backwards and forwards on their rails, and the great square metal containers slid across the boom, and ran down on chains, dangling a moment before dropping precisely into the holes ready to receive them – like teeth going into gums. As each one was placed the ship reverberated like a great gong, and rode up and down against the quay. When I thought the last one was in place and the loading completed, another layer was begun. It was like a giant child playing with building blocks, and I wondered when it would stop; soon I would not be able to see over the containers from my high deck. Fortunately the bridge and the living quarters were all up in the bows so the view of where we were headed would be unimpeded.

The afternoon light bathed the port in a silky softness, strangely at variance with the oily dirt, the bustle and the loud clamour of the place. The Pelrider was loading at an outer berth from where the heavy angularity of all the landbound things – cranes, concrete quays and railway tracks – was bordered by the formless moving ocean. It was a striking scene full of movement, and I remained watching at the rail until night fell, when it was changed and stars filled the velvety darkness on the seaward side, while on the port side white arclights cut harsh pools out of the blackness.

I was finally detached from my viewpoint by the mate summoning me to come and take my supper in the wardroom. In solitary state I had set before me boiled mutton, pasta, chips, apple, yoghurt and lager. The day before I had barely eaten a thing, and now I was being offered the equivalent of three meals in one. This is often the pattern on journeys – feasting or semi-starvation – and neither state in the least dependent on the money in my pocket, but rather on the uncertainties and lack of a fixed pattern in the way I choose to travel. As always, mindful of future lean times, I tackled everything I could. The mutton, pasta, yoghurt and lager were delicious; only the chips were eschewed, and that merely for lack of space. The handsome young Pakistani cook hovered to see I had everything I needed, bringing a fresh can of lager as soon as I had finished the first. He also insisted I take away the apple for later. The only mistake was to end the meal with more of the excellent strong coffee, fatal to sleep at that hour.

All night long I was aware of the passage of the Pelrider over a calm sea as I lay warm and relaxed in my bunk, watching the stars swing gently to and fro through the porthole. I probably dropped off from time to time, but if I did I was unaware of it. Lines from Walt Whitman's 'Passage to India' ran like a refrain through my head, 'O, further, further sail. Are they not all the seas of God?' I had the sense of having been given a short breathing space, a time out of context.

Dawn, a red sky and the mountains of Lebanon white with snow heralded Christmas Day. With the sun rising straight before us over those dazzling slopes it was useless for photographs, but I went onto the bridge and took some anyway, because the day and the place were holy, and to be travelling like this, away from the bustle of mass tourism was also very special and to be remembered.

CHAPTER THREE

Sanity in a Mad Land

Even through the captain's binoculars Beirut looked surprisingly unscathed for a city that had suffered ten years of repeated shelling and bombing. The sun sparkling on scudding white-topped waves cast the same clear light over shell-pocked walls and the few gutted ruins that were visible. The overall impression was of a fine modern city dramatically sited on a promontory beside a peerless sea. Only as we slid into the port, which early on this Christmas morning showed little sign of activity, did I feel a hint of menace in the scene, and that might equally well have been due to something I was anticipating.

The calm self-contained mood of the ship was broken the instant we tied up at the dockside. Eight officials scrambled aboard and were immediately ushered into a large room off the captain's cabin to check papers and to do whatever is required of port officials aboard cargo vessels in foreign ports. Smiles were few, while shouts and what sounded like threats flew thickly about. I caught one English phrase – 'heavy fine' – before the door closed.

After an hour of entertaining the officials the captain came to where I was sitting in the sun by my cabin door, and asked for my passport. An hour before he had been chatting happily to me on his bridge; now he looked a worried man. He said there were difficulties because the authorities at Limassol had failed to telephone about my arrival, and the immigration officials responsible for checking me into the country were not working on Christmas Day. The shipping agent was being sent to find a senior colleague who might be able to make the necessary arrangements. Would I mind being patient for a while longer?

My usual eagerness to get on with things had been somewhat

23

curbed by the attitude of the officials as well as by the derelict, neglected appearance of the port. I was able therefore quite honestly to assure the poor captain (who had quite enough on his plate without me adding to the burden) that there was no hurry at all. All the kidnappings, the massacres and the bitter violence of this country suddenly seemed very close. I was not exactly frightened but I felt distinctly apprehensive. Reading in the warm sunshine or having the workings of the Pelrider explained to me by the friendly Greek mate and the Syrian chief engineer happily delayed the moment of stepping out onto that problematic shore.

Officials kept passing and repassing, staring but saying nothing. More angry sounds from the captain's cabin, and another hour passed. The captain returned my passport, together with a large bag of books which, he said shyly, I might like. I hoped the captain was not anticipating that I would be aboard long enough to read them all. Sorting through the collection of lurid paperbacks, I found a thick John Fowles novel which I had not read and tried to decide whether I could cope with the extra weight.

I have learnt to be rigorous about everything I take on a journey, since weight is the arch-enemy of bicycling. On the flat it is not so bad, but faced with the slightest incline every ounce tells. The rule is if it isn't strictly necessary, don't take it. Clothing I keep to a minimum, just what I wear, plus one clean set of everything. This being a winter journey, however, I needed far more and heavier clothing than usual, and most of this would have to be stuffed in the panniers while I rode, since it was only the nights that I would need most of it.

A basic survival kit of sleeping bag, bivvy bag, small cooking set and emergency food made another weighty burden, which together with washing things, medicines and tools and the long list of essential bits and pieces increased significantly. Books therefore, the heaviest items of all, had to be severely limited. For this journey, a Bible was essential source material, and even a lightweight one used up what I felt was the entire book allowance. But I also needed at least one thick notebook, and the one slim volume of non-essential reading matter included

for the sake of sanity was already pushing the limits dangerously. I had read this novel twice through already, so although I
feared the thick Fowles book might well prove the proverbial
straw, I was unable to resist the temptation. I justified my decision by the fact that as it was a very battered copy I would have
no compunction about tearing off pages as I read them. By the
time it came to crossing the mountains its bulk should be considerably reduced.

I had just finished these long deliberations when the cook
summoned me down to the wardroom for Christmas lunch. I
got no further than the first companionway, however, before a
counter-order came to disembark immediately. The pace and
focus of the day changed abruptly. From my place of observer
in the wings I was shifted to centre stage, and all the shouting
and arguments now eddied around me where I stood on the
quayside. A small thin old man in a very smart suit, whom I
assumed, quite rightly, to be the senior shipping agent, seized
my panniers and stuffed them hurriedly into the boot of his car,
waving me to sit up front. I hung back waiting for Roberts
which a sailor was bringing down the gangplank. Several of the
officials were pulling at my arms, attempting to give me conflicting orders.

I seemed to be the only person not shouting and gesticulat-
ing, but with all around me so steamed up I wondered how
much longer my patience would hold. Eventually some sort of
order was restored, and the agent drove off along the quay with
my baggage, while I rode behind, pedalling furiously in my
efforts to keep up, and trying to wave farewell to the crew of
the Pelrider at the same time. After a very tiring sprint along
deserted quays made perilous by gaping pot-holes and wheel-
trapping rusting rail lines, we stopped at some dilapidated
buildings.

Here I was hustled through a succession of doorways in
order that haughty men could cast a supercilious glance at my
passport before waving me on to someone else. Another spate
of shouting broke out about who should grace the despised
document with an official stamp.

When the agent finally returned my panniers and I loaded up

Roberts, I thought I was now free to go, but the instant I swung my leg thankfully over the crossbar I was surrounded by yet another posse of uniformed men, about a dozen of them pressing in on me from all sides. Men began opening the panniers behind me, while others rummaged about in my handlebar bag and through the front panniers. I was still astride Roberts so it was impossible to watch what everyone was up to. They were quite unlike any customs officials I had come across, and I was alarmed. If they wanted to search my luggage that was all right by me but it should be done at a table, preferably inside, where I could keep a proper eye on the proceedings.

In retrospect I realize they were looking for a bribe, and that their provoking behaviour was geared to that end. At the time I was too busy concentrating on protecting the obvious valuables like documents, currency and the like to think of anything else. In any case I am no good at all about bribes and always ignore signs that suggest they might be welcome.

One of the men undid the small toolbag that sits under Roberts' saddle, and took out the carefully rolled spare inner tube. He unwound it completely, grinning at me when I protested, and then tossed it on the ground together with the tools. Another dropped a small perfume flask (another of my few luxuries) smashing the plastic casing. At that point I felt the proceedings had got right out of hand. Everyone had some piece of my equipment in his hand, and unless I was going to become really angry I realized the moment had come to drop the patience and diplomacy I had been assiduously practising since daybreak.

My temper can I fear be rather fierce and it is something I therefore usually try to keep on a tight rein. But if I jump the gun at times like these, rather than waiting for the explosion, I can often act a simulated anger which is far more effective and certainly more predictable than the real thing. I did this now. I got off Roberts, took out my notebook and informed them coldly that I was writing down everything they had done and said to me, and that an account of their disgraceful treatment of a visitor to their country would appear in all the major Western newspapers. They would be in dead trouble I told them. And having said it in English, I repeated it in French, and stamped my foot a bit to add emphasis to the words. As it was all absolute nonsense, of course, it must have been my sudden change of attitude that did the trick, for I had no more trouble from them after that. One or two tried to bluff it out, protesting they were doing no more than their duty, but most looked suitably contrite, and several of them even apologized and helped me to gather up my scattered possessions.

The agent whom I had assumed had long since departed was in fact waiting at a discreet distance to learn the fate of his company's temporary guest. It seemed to me to imply that I had acquitted myself with credit, for he shook my hand warmly and escorted me to the main road, before hurrying off to resume his interrupted Christmas.

The main north-south Lebanese highway at which he left me resembled nothing so much as a vision of hell, a view that I subsequently found no cause to revise. Lebanon has only a narrow coastal strip, and the wide highway, innocent of any white lines to separate the six lanes, seemed to me to take up most of the space between the mountains and the sea. Nothing else appeared to exist except a great river of rushing cars with a heavy pall of pollution hanging above them and a cacophony of blaring horns and engine roar that blighted the brain, rendering it incapable of coherent thought. I had not planned in which order I would explore Lebanon. I had vaguely thought to spend the night in Beirut, follow up some introductions there and find out what was happening generally before setting off. But so daunting was the prospect before me that I simply pedalled off in the direction I was facing, which happened to be north, towards Byblos.

For the next three hours I felt I was fighting for my very life, which of course was nonsense. My life was in far more competent hands: it was my guardian angel who had his work cut out. During the years of civil war cars had become so cheap in the Lebanon that everyone could own at least one of them. All of these cars, in varying states of decrepitude, were on the road on this Christmas Day, and the majority were going north. White lines would probably not have helped. Driving techniques would doubtless have remained the same whatever the conditions. Cars swooped from lane to lane on the instant, whenever a temporary check occurred or a sudden whim took them.

Traffic indicators seemed not to be in fashion. Drivers announced their change of direction only after the event, with a triumphal blaring of the horn. Any car leaving the main highway on one of the many sliproads would cut across my bows like the relentless scythe of the Grim Reaper himself. For the three hours it took to reach Byblos where I was at last able to extricate myself from the maelstrom, Scott's words from the Antarctic stayed with me: 'This is an awful place.'

Byblos was one of the cities of the ancient world I had long wished to visit, yet arriving there, all I was aware of for some time was the sheer bliss of being clear of the rushing, roaring river of choking fumes. There had been little opportunity to take in much on the ride because all my concentration was needed for survival. Nonetheless images inevitably register themselves upon the consciousness, and much more so when cycling. There had been ribbon development the whole way alongside the highway, filling in whatever space was left between the mountains and the sea. At best the architecture appeared to be no more than brutally functional. Whenever the road rose sufficiently for the sea to come into view across the line of buildings, it seemed shockingly real in comparison with the rotting concrete, a powerful untamed force – dark and intensely blue.

The ruins of Byblos produced a similar shock, again largely because of the contrast with the awful buildings that surrounded it. Like Beirut, the city of Byblos was beautifully sited on a promontory rising gently from the sea. There is nothing remotely intact in the ruins beyond the Crusader castle and a Roman temple, both of which are relatively modern in relation to the old Phoenician city itself. But the overall impression is of rightness and harmony, an effect largely achieved by the warm reddish stone out of which everything is built, from the vast ancient perimeter walls, the temple platforms, elaborate tombs and palaces, to the re-used material of the great square castle.

Enhanced by the green of the many palms and semi-tropical plants scattered throughout the site, the towering snow-capped mountains behind, and the spectacular sea in front, it is a scene of exotic richness. Add to this the fact that I was seeing it for the first time against a sky gorgeously flushed by the setting sun, and with the impassioned cry of a muezzin coming in broken threads of sound from a distant minaret, and all the romance, the beauty and the mystery of travel lay before me.

Hard though it was to tear myself away, further exploration had to wait; the first thing was to get myself organized. I had not eaten since breakfast; I had not felt safe enough on that hellish road even to take a drink from my water bottle, and my throat still burned from the exhaust fumes. Somewhere I had read that there was a very special camping site near to Byblos – the only camping place in Lebanon – and I set about looking for it while the daylight lasted.

I found it a little north of Byblos in the unprepossessing out-skirts of a village which had grown up around it. Compared with camping sites in Europe, Amchit des Colombs was rather drab and rundown. In relation to the rest of battle-scarred Lebanon, however, it was a little paradise, and in more ways than those of which I was immediately aware. I had no tent, but there were cabins and apartments to rent, and while I was attempting to negotiate the price of one of these from the rather obtuse Egyptian youth in charge, a Lebanese man who introduced himself as Samir came to my aid. The owner, he told me in French, was visiting relatives but would soon return, in the meantime I was welcome to come and take tea with him beside his caravan.

Samir had brought the caravan from Germany, where he travelled frequently on his import business – most people in Lebanon, I would soon discover, seemed to be in the import business – though I never did meet anyone who exported which perplexed me rather. The caravan was fully equipped for cooking and sleeping, and before I had finished even the first cup of tea Samir offered me the use of it for the next day or two. He and his wife used it only at weekends, he said; during the week they lived in their flat in the suburbs of Beirut. In case

I should feel uncomfortable about his offer, he hastened to tell me a little about the purpose of Amchit des Colombs.

It had been started by a member of a wealthy local family who made a strip of his coastal lands available to scholars and travellers visiting Byblos, for at the time there was nowhere to stay in the vicinity. As the place had gradually evolved into a regular campsite the village of Amchit had expanded and now pressed in upon it on three sides. The present owners, a daughter and son-in-law of the original founders, had built the place up as a business. Like many Lebanese, they had links abroad and had taken their young family to France during the worst years of the troubles. Returning before the country was anything like stable, they had decided to make Amchit des Colombs into a safe haven, firstly for Lebanese people and more recently for the foreign tourists who were just beginning to return to the Lebanon.

Somehow the owners had been able to establish the camp as the only 'no arms zone' in Lebanon. Even the police and the army had to leave their weapons at the gate. Everyone using the camp, residents and visitors, had to conform to civilized standards of behaviour or they were asked to leave. It was wonderful here, said Samir, a place to relax among friends and forget the troubles. He urged me again to accept his offer adding that I could check with Pascal and François, the owners of the camp, whose house was in the centre of the site.

After meeting Pascal and several of his other guests, I was more than happy to stay, and looked forward to taking up the many invitations to talk over coffee. One of the strangest Christmas Days I have ever spent ended with a solitary feast of delicious take-away chicken, followed by a refreshing shower, the hot water for which was obtained by lighting a fire of palm fronds under a slim boiler in an outhouse.

My sense of well being complete, I read the office of Compline and went to bed clad in my thermals and with all the blankets I could find over my lightweight sleeping bag. Words I had just read – 'Thou hast put gladness in my heart' – seemed very fitting to the day. So far all the difficulties of the journey had been resolved by the warm kindness of people rather than anything I had been able to do. I was not only glad but profoundly thankful, and had a warm sense of being cared for.

A golden dawn flushed with rosy pink heralded the feast day of St Stephen. The magic of the open sea fronting the camp transcended the mean encroaching suburbs of the village. I went down first thing to explore Phoenician Byblos, the town where the name Christianity was first coined. Never had the proto-martyr of the Christian faith seemed more real than in this lovely antique setting among the platforms and the columns of pagan temples. I sat in the shade and read again the account of his martyrdom in Acts, preceded as it was by his long dissertation on the history of the Jews that had led from Abraham to the passion and triumph of Christ. Even as he speaks the tremendous meaning of what he is saying seems to strike Stephen afresh. 'His face,' writes the chronicler, 'was like the face of an angel.'

Over the next few days I used the camp as a base and explored Lebanon up as far as Tripoli and the borders. It was a confusing scene and difficult to know who was really in control of the country. The Israelis held their 'security strip' in the south, from which they still regularly shelled Lebanese territory in the name of controlling Muslim militants. In the north and east, Syrian soldiers were everywhere, operating roadblocks and administering various aspects of Lebanese life. It was easy to see why many Lebanese claimed Syria would never relinquish their hold on a country they had always claimed was historically theirs.

I had never really understood what had brought about the dreadful internecine warfare in Lebanon. Nor did being there and talking to a wide variety of people, both in the camp and outside, make the matter any clearer. Older people tended to say it had been largely a war of religion and talked of the 'Muslim invasion' in which a ninety per cent Christian country had become fifty per cent Muslim in barely a decade. But clearly it was more complicated than that. There were factions within factions, both in the Christian and the Muslim populations, and with many outside forces and powers involved.

The whole issue was further complicated by hundreds of

years of turbulent history. More kingdoms had risen and fallen in the Middle East, more empires had held their successive sway there than anywhere else in the world. The division of the area into states and countries after the First World War had brought about the collapse of the corrupt and run-down Ottoman Empire was no easy task. With the best will in the world, lines drawn with rulers on a map do not guarantee future stability. As one old Lebanese ex-Admiral was later to tell me, the most stable countries in the Middle East were those with a strong leadership, like Syria and Jordan. A democracy like Lebanon which tried to write into its constitution an equal share of power for all parties ends up in anarchy.

Most people, however, were no longer interested in analysing what had gone wrong; it was the present that concerned them. Even the salient issue of whether the peace would hold or not was dulled by a great weariness with war. There was a general resentment and anger about the continued shelling by Israel, and the high-profile presence of the Syrians, both of which demonstrated Lebanon's subjectivity, but it was easier and less painful to pretend to ignore it.

In an attempt to show me a different face of Lebanon, Pascal took me on a tour of the original pretty village of Amchit high above the sea and graced with fine churches and the elegant expansive houses of her various relatives, a little shabby now but a world away from the modern gimcrack concrete buildings. She also took me for a drive up into the mountains, past the abandoned terraces and the summer villages, to glimpse the remains of the great cedar forests of Lebanon. These had once spread over the mountains of Lebanon for mile after mile. They even figure in the Gilgamesh myth and the Bible is full of references to them. Their precious timber graced the King's house in Jerusalem, its fragrant luxury thought by the prophets to be a sign of Israel's decadence. 'Do you think you are a king just because you build in cedar?' thunders Jeremiah, sounding yet again the old prophetic cry for the restoration of justice and righteousness as the basis of kingship. It is a sad little remnant of this forest that remains though the cry for justice and righteousness still echoes all around the war-torn region.

Of the people I met in Amchit, Sylva, a young Armenian psychology student from Beirut was the most entertaining. Full of life and poor as a church mouse, she somehow managed to scrape together the money to rent a one-roomed apartment in the camp, and spent every moment she could there, claiming that Amchit preserved her sanity. She was supporting herself through university by teaching part-time, but clearly it was a struggle, though not one she allowed to get her down. Part of the reason I enjoyed Sylva's company was that her English was excellent which meant I could give my awful, ungrammatical French a rest. As it was holiday time Sylva invited some of her sixth-form students, also Armenian, to spend a day with her, and suggested I might like to meet them.

I don't know whether at eighteen I would have been fascinated by a middle-aged female touring foreign lands with a bicycle. But these girls had grown up in a world of great violence, and coming from a people that had already learned to protect its own and preserve its social structures, they had undoubtedly led more sheltered and circumscribed lives than I had at their age. Interest from the young is always flattering, but I would have enjoyed the company of these eight young girls anyway. They seemed so natural, so untouched by the pseudo-sophistication of the West and yet were by no means short of intelligent comment. Most complained that they were not allowed enough freedom. But while they seemed full of a touching eagerness to experience life more fully, they also seemed to accept the good sense behind their parents' strictures. They were proud of their identity both as Armenians and Lebanese and seemed confident of the future.

Seeing my interest they begged me to come and visit them in their 'ghetto'. One of their number, Rita, quite rightly thought I would gain a far better understanding if I explored the Armenian quarter of Beirut, Bourj Hammoud, under their guidance. Their enthusiasm for the scheme caught fire and drew me along with it. They would get hold of bicycles and join me for the last part of the ride, they said, and I found myself promising to meet them in two days' time outside a sandwich shop on the outskirts of Beirut.

CHAPTER FOUR

Beirut

South to Beirut proved no less chaotic and frightening an experience than the ride northwards. Only by adopting something of the fatalistic attitude to life of those around me was it bearable, though a series of sickening collisions made such sang-froid hard to maintain. Not far from the meeting place there was another incident, this time involving me. I was just preparing to do battle with the driver of the car which had forced me off the road, only to find that the aggressor was a young man bent on offering nothing more offensive than hospitality. A keen cyclist himself and a graduate of an English university, he had spotted me with my laden panniers and had waited for a suitable opportunity to get me to stop. He hoped he hadn't startled me too much, he said, but you had to act quickly on that road. His father would never forgive him if he missed the chance of inviting me home; travellers were all too rare in Lebanon these days. I had only to say the word and he would load Roberts onto his roof rack and drive me up the mountains to his parents' house.

Such chance encounters are part of the delights of travel, and any other time I would have been glad to accept his offer and glimpse another stratum of Lebanese life. But I was on my way to the rendezvous with the Armenian students and did not know what my plans would be thereafter. He left me his card in case I failed to make contact with the Armenians or needed his help in any way. As things turned out, I did not see him again, but he provided an introduction that enabled me to visit the area south of Beirut.

Rita, Sylva and the rest of the escort of bright-faced Armenian girls were awaiting me when, more by luck than judgement, I managed to pull off the ribbon of death at the appointed felafel stand at the northern end of Beirut.

Over the next few days I was to come to know the run-down, desperately overcrowded quarter of Bourj Hammoud which was occupied almost exclusively by Armenians. Noisy and polluted as it was, it had nothing at all to commend it except for the people, and they made it very special indeed.

I was already aware of the role that the Armenians of Bourj Hammoud had played in Lebanon's civil war, but although it reflects greatly to their credit no one there ever tried to tell me about it. Indeed it was difficult to get them to talk at all about the war years. Like most Lebanese they wanted to put the past behind them and get on with rebuilding the country.

The Armenians did not get involved in the fighting at all, but they stopped at nothing to protect their own people and their quarter. If an Armenian was killed, three of the faction responsible would be dead by the following morning. Because of its reputation and the security it afforded, Bourj Hammoud became the only safe corridor for the waves of refugees, both Muslim and Christian, that poured through the city after the various massacres and reprisals.

Armenians are a unique people. Like the Jews, they too have suffered a terrible genocide within living memory. Eighty years ago the Turks wiped out several million of them, a third of their number, in mass killings and torture, and in wholesale death-marches of unbelievable cruelty and barbarity. But whereas the entire world is aware of the Jewish Holocaust, and some attempts at reparation have been made for it by Germany, Turkey has never been called to account for the Armenian genocide, nor has it even acknowledged it happened.

Naturally enough this is a continuing cause of hurt and bitterness for Armenians, as too is their exile from the lands of Eastern Turkey which they and their ancestors inhabited continuously for thousands of years. With such an unenviable history it would perhaps be understandable if their hearts had been hardened to the sufferings of others. But the strong social cohesion and racial memories of the Armenians are firmly based on Christian principles which have prevented them adopting exclusivist attitudes.

Armenia has the distinction of being the very first country to adopt Christianity as its official religion, so the compassion of modern Armenians for others is of course fitting; it is also very rare.

Bourj Hammoud was certainly not lovely. Many of the buildings were shell-pocked, cracked and shabby. Services were barely functioning if at all. Water was scarce, the supply intermittent and of poor quality. Hundreds of generators producing electricity on a small scale added to the terrible air and noise pollution. Only the telephone seemed unaffected and in a country so dedicated to trading that was of course the main priority. A start had been made on restoring other services and many roads had been dug up and were ankle deep in mud from leaking pipes. Not that any road was any better than a hazardous obstacle course, rendering walking a slow and tiring business. But even in these impossible conditions cars occupied nearly every inch of space, belching exhaust fumes like so many bad-tempered dragons frustrated at being able to move neither forwards nor backwards.

In such grid-lock situations the bicycle is usually king, but not in Bourj Hammoud where even the narrow pavements had been usurped by parked vehicles. During my stay, which extended to the best part of a week, I was thankful to leave Roberts in a garage belonging to Rita's uncle.

The extensive tour of such worthy institutions as churches, emergency health centres, schools and colleges which my well-meaning youthful guides had thought suitable was thankfully got through in one single exhausting day. After that I could begin to flesh out this basic picture of a caring community that had weathered a prolonged and violent storm. It was the girls themselves who intrigued me. Children of a war that had raged for seventeen years, they had never known a time when their country was not in a mess. All of them were coming up to eighteen and would soon be going to university. Intelligent and well-educated, they were also unworldly and possessed a refreshing air of eagerness and a confidence in the future that sat oddly with their country's recent history and likely future.

Yet on reflection it did not seem so odd. As a small child growing up in World War II, I too had no concept of war as being other than the normal state of affairs. From my limited experience it seemed that life had always been like that. Intelligent young people brought up in the suburbs of Belfast told me they were so used to reports of bombings and to the presence of soldiers on the streets that they said it took something like the killing of someone they knew to bring the reality of the situation home to them.

When pressed, Rita and her friends could remember times of being very frightened during prolonged shelling or when the worst of the Israeli bombing of Beirut took place, but in the scale of things all that was a long time ago. Poised as they were on the threshold of adulthood, eager to try their wings, their childhood was further behind them now than it would ever seem again.

It was clear to see where the strength and balance of these young people had sprung from. It was the parents who had paid the price. There were many sad and obvious casualties of Lebanon's war, but after a few days in Beirut I realized that no adult had escaped entirely unscathed. Armenians had concentrated on seeing that children were as little affected as possible and perhaps this focus, together with the solidarity of the community had helped them to survive the worst. Education had been maintained, ambitions fostered, standards preserved, although at times it must have been nearly impossible.

After the chaotic mess and dirt of the streets, Bourj Hammoud homes were miracles of order and cleanliness; a contrast that never ceased to astonish me. Beirut homes are on the whole very small because the city is so overcrowded, doubly so since the war. All except the poorest people have a second home in the mountain villages, because the coastal plain becomes so very hot in the summer months. Rita's flat in a faceless five-floor concrete block was typical of many I visited. With only two bedrooms for the five people who lived there, ingenuity and order was employed to conquer the chronic shortage of space. So small was it that the kitchen, no more than a large cupboard, had to be vacated in order for anyone to get into the shoe box of a bathroom. Rita's bedroom which she shared with her older brother and sister had just room enough for a double bunk, a single bed and a small wardrobe. To dress they had to scatter to various corners of the flat. Maintaining the uncluttered look, while cooking elaborate meals, washing clothes and doing all the necessary household chores was a work of art as well as unrelenting effort, and yet I never heard a voice raised or a cross word spoken in that household.

The cohesion and warmth of Armenian society was apparent in the stream of neighbours, family and friends calling in during this holiday season. It was an atmosphere in which I felt instantly at home. Shortage of room in Armenian homes notwithstanding, I was offered my pick of places to stay. Rita's mother even urged me to consider her sitting-room sofa, a kindness I found deeply moving. Since I had a choice, I opted for a room of my own in the apartment of a young Armenian artist and his young girlfriend, whose beautifully poised head on its long slender neck could well have been modelled by Modigliani.

This apartment was in an older, more French-looking building, and belonged to the young man's father, a gifted and established painter whose atelier was below. The free room was a temporary store for piles of dusty books and magazines and forgotten artists' props and nick-nacks, for the Torossian family had spent most of the last decade in Paris and were still not fully settled back into Beirut life. The large sofa bed in the centre of all this flotsam became my oasis from the currents of destruction and chaos that could still be felt lurking in this troubled country. In spite of the urgings of the senior Torossians for me to sleep in their uniquely large and far more civilized apartment, the temporary nature of this lodging seemed more in keeping with the general conditions of Beirut, and I stayed put.

Young Stephan Torossian's paintings, with which the flat was filled, were nothing like his father's. Where Torossian Senior painted light and form in a manner reminiscent of the impressionists, his son's works were all violence and struggle, though equally gifted and probably more inventive. He earned his living making illustrations for French comics of the apocalyptic science fiction order, cartoons as violent in character as his more serious work.

Unlike my other young friends, Stephan was aware of the effect the war had made on him before his father had taken him to France. As a result he had spent his French school-days in a special class for disruptive children who had been similarly traumatized. Very intelligent and widely read, all Stephan's canvases seemed to be a working out of his inner conflicts. They were essays on man's destructive forces and his possibilities for redemption. Dark, heavy canvases, challenging and full of a terrifying energy but possessed also with tenderness and a young man's optimism. Somehow they reminded me of his countryman, Kahlil Gibran, to whose shrine in the mountains above Tripoli I had paid a hurried visit.

While exploring the life of Beirut, I was also thinking about going south to Tyre and Sidon and beyond them to the Israeli 'security' zone. I had originally wanted to cycle this way continuing down the coast into Israel. From all I heard in Beirut I realized that no one was allowed anywhere near this usurped region and that there was not a chance that the Israelis would allow me through the border. This made me all the more determined to see what I could of the area before leaving Lebanon by the mountain route: how to do it was the question.

Usually a bicycle is an ideal low profile means of getting through troubled places. By choosing the right moment I have pedalled through several war zones in far greater safety than if I had been travelling in a coveted vehicle. This occasion was different, as were the forces involved and the nature of the conflict. After drawing blanks over going it alone, I phoned the number given me by the young motorist who had wanted to take me to his parents' home in the mountains.

Two days later I was picked up as arranged and driven south.

Jani, whose car it was, was a Muslim, and at first he refused even to accept money for petrol. He said it was his duty to show me what had been done to his country; the more people who knew the facts, the more hope for justice. He was not a comfortable companion, but he was reliable and he knew a great deal about the complicated, messy politics of the Middle East, far more in fact than I could absorb.

The Phoenician towns of Sidon and Tyre should have been the high points of this route. More than four thousand years they had stood there, with fleets bustling in and out of their ports carrying trade goods to and from the furthest reaches of the known world. The Phoenicians were always great traders, ones who knew their markets. Tyrian purple had dyed cloth for the robes of Roman emperors. One of Tyre's kings, Hiram, had supplied the cedar wood and the craftsmen to build a palace for David when he first became king of Israel. Later still he built the Temple of Jerusalem for David's son, Solomon.

All these ancient dealings are carefully recorded and cross-referenced in the Old Testament books of Kings, Samuel and Chronicles. The account of the preparation for the building of Jerusalem's first temple in 1 Kings 5:1 strikes a touching note: 'And Hiram king of Tyre sent his servants unto Solomon; for he had heard that they had anointed him king in the room of his father: for Hiram was ever a lover of David.'

In the light of Jani's feelings about modern Israel the words were doubly poignant, for he held Israel entirely responsible, not only for the horrors that had befallen Lebanon, but for all the problems of the Middle East. 'In the end,' he told me, 'Lebanon will be the sacrifice for Israel's peace. We will be given to Syria as the spoils of war.' This was not the first time I had heard this idea expressed. But remembering the lines about Hiram and his love of David, what occurred to me was that so far on this journey I had heard not one single word in praise or exoneration of Israel or its leaders.

The spell of fine weather had broken before we left Beirut. It was wet and bleak; cold by day as well as night. I wore everything I had as the car's heater was not working. The plan was to motor down by the sea route as far as we could get to the border and return through the Chouf Mountains.

It was not my kind of travelling. At the best of times I do not like cars, and this was not the best of times. I saw virtually nothing of ancient Tyre and Sidon, only brief sightings of a Crusader castle in the sea and scraps of Roman and Byzantine masonry against a lowering sullen sky. What I did gain was a general idea of the lay of the land, a feeling of the topography and a few snapshot impressions to add three-dimensional meaning to the complicated events that had been played out there.

The whole area wore the bleak appearance of disruption, from the frequency of refugee camps and the high military presence to the dirt and detritus blowing about the unkempt, broken streets of towns that had once been rich in foreign tourism. The further south we went the emptier the countryside grew. The semi-deserted villages of the lovely Chouf Mountains sat oddly with the intensively terraced hillsides and gentle pastoral scenery. Everywhere there seemed to be an air of defeat and dejection, alien to the Lebanese reputation for vigour and the ability to bounce back from reverses.

The car radio, tuned to an Arabic station ground out an endless emotive stream of what sounded like a fanatical harangue, either religious or political, which I had no idea, but on and on it went without let up, adding to the general mood of dejection. Whether Jani's gloomy predictions were right or not, they seemed in keeping with the Lebanon I was seeing, a country that had become an inevitable and unwilling victim.

Lebanon's troubles really began with the expulsion of the Palestinian guerillas from Jordan. As the one remaining Arab country close enough to their homeland from which the PLO could continue their fight for international recognition, Lebanon's fate was sealed. The Lebanese state with its delicate political balance between parties and factions was simply not strong enough to keep the Palestinians out. In the face of the Israeli reprisals against Palestinian guerilla activities it soon found itself even more helpless. From there it was but a short step to chaos and civil war, helped along by the bizarre and destructive alliances between strong outside powers and the various groups and parties within.

These years of civil war left some fifty thousand Lebanese dead and created over a million refugees. Their sad patchwork camps were scattered throughout the length and breadth of the country. As in all such wars atrocities had been legion; everyone had their own tales of horror, and Jani regaled me with some of his as we drove, shouting to be heard above the endless impassioned radio tirade. What price healing with memories such as these?

Even as we drove the sound of Israeli gunfire pounding away at some poor camp suspected of harbouring terrorists or selected for a reprisal attack was a grim reminder that the conflict was by no means ended. Jani's only comment on the bombardment was: 'If you have strong friends like America, you can do whatever you want.'

Back in Beirut, in the comparative sanity of Bourj Hammoud I celebrated New Year's Eve with about thirty of Rita's family. One of her aunts had a flat with rooms whose folding doors could be opened up to accommodate such a crowd. The rooms had been emptied of their usual furniture to make space for the supper table which was made up of several small ones brought from various households and laid end to end. The bright festive cloths that covered them were all but hidden under a vast array of dishes that the women had been preparing for days past. Children, round-eyed and expectant, went around and around the table solemnly taking it all in. Outside on the balcony overlooking the ruined street the men cooked kebabs to add to the Armenian dishes of stuffed aubergines, peppers, vine leaves, salads, rice and chicken dishes.

It was a lovely party in which everyone ate enormous quantities, the men washing it down with Black Label whisky, the women and children with Coca-Cola. But at midnight when we toasted one another there was still enough Black Label for a generous tot all round.

In deference to their guest English had been spoken extensively all evening; there were few of these people, even the poorest of them who did not speak several languages, a fact that as always, made me ashamed of my own linguistic inadequacies. Before I left, one of the uncles who was a church deacon asked me how I had liked Lebanon. I thought he meant the general state of the place and I said that whereas I had enjoyed the people very much I found the country itself was rather a mess at present. 'But,' he said seriously, 'you must remember this is the Holy Land.'

'Why holy?' I asked, a bit fuddled with Black Label by this time, 'Because of God's promise?'

'No,' he replied, 'because the feet of Christ walked this land. Look to the heart not to the place.'

The deacon's words were fair comment. The most important thing that visiting Lebanon had shown me was a people who had been subjected to a long and violent storm but had not been defeated by it. They had weathered it, I thought by living by simple principles of Christian love. It was indeed the heart and not the land that would be my abiding memory of Lebanon.

CHAPTER FIVE

Over the Mountains
to Damascus

I left Beirut by bus, meekly agreeing with my Lebanese hosts that the bicycle was no more suitable for this stage of my journey than it had been for the brief foray into Southern Lebanon. Their fears were for my safety, mine had more to do with the weather. During the last days of the old year another thick snowfall had wiped out the road to Syria, and although New Year's Day saw it open to traffic once again, it seemed foolish to risk icy conditions on the steep slopes of the Lebanon and Anti-Lebanon Mountains. And in any case, with Roberts so grossly over-laden the two huge ascents would not have been much fun.

It was still dark when we pulled out of Beirut, and the passengers who, due to the capricious timetable, had been waiting several hours for the bus settled down at once to sleep. I was grateful for the quiet and the lack of lighting because I was feeling anything but dry-eyed after the last of the series of emotional leave-takings from my new Armenian friends. In a final act of kindness Rita and her father had picked me up with their Land Rover at 5 a.m. in order to spare me a difficult journey through the winding streets and the hassle of getting Roberts stowed aboard the bus.

Grinding up the endless steep bends of the first mountain range, shells of abandoned, broken buildings loomed like spectres out of the bleak grey dawn. Piles of rubbish and debris, the scars of war, were everywhere, smudging and defacing the ancient beauty of the land. I found myself thinking of Jeremiah's prophecies written two and a half thousand years ago in which he predicts the downfall of nations who had delighted in Israel's conquest by the Babylonians. The horror of what had happened to Lebanon could so easily be fitted into the context of Jeremiah's curses, especially considering the central role that modern Israel had played in the destruction. From there was but a step to the image of the vengeful God of the Old Testament; ideas that are still common currency in this part of the world.

Just as we reached the summit of the Mount Lebanon range the sun rose above the further Anti-Lebanon Mountains, and immediately the grey drifts of snow on either side were lit with a rosy splendour. The lovely lines of the terraced hillsides stood out in sharp relief and the day was transformed. The respite was brief. Almost immediately we were engulfed in a thick grey mist that filled the Bekaa Valley, and only occasional wayside buildings of a depressing ugliness punctuated the gloom.

The long narrow Bekaa forms the northern end of the great Rift Valley which continues southwards right down through Africa, by way of the Jordan and the Dead Sea. I have travelled much of this great cleft in the earth's surface, and I felt cheated at seeing so little of this stretch of it. My one comfort was that in these conditions I would have gained no clearer impression of it by bicycle.

We rose above the grey cotton wool during the ascent of the Anti-Lebanon with the abruptness of an aeroplane climbing out of the clouds. As though the sun was the common signal, everyone in the bus began to stir at the same time, stretching and tidying themselves in preparation for the border crossings. A young man in the seat opposite started a conversation with me. He was very excited, he confided, because today he was to have his long-awaited interview at the American Embassy in Damascus to see if he would be allowed in as an immigrant. He showed me the thick form all filled in, and I am sure that if I had displayed the least inclination he would have gone through all the answers with me, point by point. He said he had applied for entry to country after country, including Britain, all without success. The war had scattered his family and he could not bear the thought of having to remain in Lebanon for the rest of his life. There was nothing here for him! He had been in Sweden for some years as a refugee, and when the worst of the danger was judged to be over, and they had sent him back, he said he had felt like killing himself. America was his last hope. I wished him luck.

The Lebanese and the Syrian crossing posts were near the summit of the Anti-Lebanon. With memories of my previous passage through Syria ten years before I expected long delays at this border, but the heavy-handed official harassment of Westerners in force at that time seemed to be a thing of the past. The ritual of not being allowed in until a hundred dollars had been turned into Syrian currency at a ruinous rate of exchange was also in abeyance so there was no need to force travellers to wait for hours, or even all night, for the bank to open. To my surprise I was duly processed and my passport stamped if not exactly with friendliness, at least with a degree of efficiency and tolerance.

With both crossing posts behind me and with the sun now shining warmly on a road that showed little trace of snow or ice I decided to leave the bus and bicycle on down to Damascus. A wise decision it proved, for the bus broke down not much further on and when I passed it the driver and his mate were busy under the bonnet looking for the cause. I hoped the young man would not be made late for his appointment at the American Embassy.

Once I was up and pedalling, swinging along an empty road, and singing from sheer elation, I realized how much I had missed this sort of freedom and peace, this sense of harmony with nature. In the crowded confines of Beirut I had almost forgotten such feelings exist. I love cities and the excitement they offer – particularly the music, theatre, art and architecture. But for the sensation of being one hundred per cent alive and awake to the joy and wonder of creation, riding a good bicycle along the summit of a mountain road on a sunny day takes a lot of beating.

I did not have long to enjoy my solitude. Halfway through 'The heavens are telling the glory of God' I had Damascus in full view below me, a shimmering white city on the level Syrian Plain. It had expanded since I saw it last with miles of apricot orchards and gardens swallowed up in extensive, smart new suburbs. I wondered how long it would be before the oasis on which this very ancient city was founded would be entirely hidden under concrete. I would have loved to have come upon it like the nineteenth century travellers when it was in the heart of the desert and entirely surrounded by green waving fronds.

Once I was down among the bustling mêlée of traffic I had more pressing concerns to think about, though compared with Beirut the roads of Damascus are a model of order and sobriety. The streets are wide and well-planned, with adequate pavements and traffic lights that work and are obeyed. There is also a sufficient variety of architecture (though much of it depressingly lacking in style) to make finding one's way a simple task. The driving is also surprisingly restrained by Middle Eastern standards. It is only the many cyclists who could be described as anarchic, and this is simply because most of them prefer to ride on the wrong side of the road against the traffic. (Actually this method of progression is really much safer for cyclists than riding with the traffic, as in a contraflow system the rider can be seen more easily and is in less danger of being mown down from behind, but it is a method that tends to scare drivers and other cyclists who are not used to it.) Since this was the accepted method of bicycling in Damascus I adopted it too for the few days I was there.

Damascus itself seemed to me to be a far more prosperous and modern city than I remembered, though not until I came to the walls of the old city itself, the Hellenic Roman city of Damascus did I feel the familiar thrill of recognition. Nothing had changed here at all. This was the very city to which Paul had come when he was still Saul and blind from his encounter with the Risen Christ. I had arrived at the entrance to the long suq that leads to the Vicus Rectus, the 'Street called Straight'.

I knew of nowhere to stay inside the ancient walls so I booked into the first cheap little hotel I found nearby. It was called 'The Grand' and from the comings and goings later on I suspected it was probably a brothel. The immediate area was full of such places. But it being out of season and not at all busy the management was happy enough to let me bargain for a large airy room on the top floor with a view of the sky across the rooftops. It would not have been a happy choice for a long stay in warm weather since the wash-basin had long been without a complete trap and emptied most of its contents into a greasy bucket beneath. Also the numerous pipes that festooned the room were hung with more spiders' webs than I would have believed possible, and the bedding was definitely suspect. But with the aid of my camping gear I was comfortable enough there for a few nights, and no one bothered me.

The staff were kindness itself, carrying Roberts up and down the many flights of stairs whenever I came in or out and often refusing a tip for the service. They were always offering me free cups of tea, too, whenever I collected my key. Tea was always on the go for the male guests who seemed to sit about all day watching television in the hall. The only drawback to 'The Grand' really, apart from the spiders, sinks and beds, was the fearful noise from the traffic that hurtles around the walls of Old Damascus, and from the vendors who swarmed on the pavements below selling every commodity that could be imagined, though specializing in low-cost radios. Whoever said the English are a nation of shopkeepers should have first visited Damascus. There was no question of there being room to walk on these pavements, it was difficult even forcing a path through the vendors spilling onto the road.

There was little time to savour this rich low-life area, it simply washed over me as I slept. The endlessly fascinating world of the walled city drew me no less than it had on the first occasion I came there. In fact this time it seemed more approachable, more open, possibly because it was out of season and there were almost no other visitors. The beauty of the city after Beirut was most marked particularly in the rough domestic architecture of the streets. The small overhanging balconies with their endless variety of shape and decoration gave me an almost permanent crick in the neck. I became aware that the city was full of minarets, both great and minor ones, and that no two were quite the same shape or ever embellished like any other.

An extraordinary world lay behind many of the deceptively blank-walled alleyways of Damascus. I would glimpse a flash of opulence behind some inconspicuous wooden door left half-ajar; push it open and find myself in a sumptuous courtyard of yet another palace that was being refurbished. These palaces often spread over a considerable area, yet no notion of their presence could be gained from walking the winding passage-ways outside. Within were gardens of orange trees, patterned marble courts with tinkling fountains, arbours roofed by wonderful filigree ceilings and suites of rooms whose only fur-nishings were the ornate magnificence of the walls. Had there not been such a spate of restoration I probably would never have seen these gems of Damascene architecture. As it was, a modest tip to a workman and I was free to wander about them at my leisure.

Down through the centre of the maze of Damascus as in all Hellenistic cities was an arrow-straight wide central way with raised colonnades on either side and space in the centre for chariots. This central thoroughfare is still basically the same today only narrower now and without the colonnading. At one end lies the Suq el Tawil, the Long Suq, an exciting cavernous thoroughfare with numerous lesser suqs leading off it. The high vaulted iron roof is pierced with innumerable pinholes through which glints of the brilliant Syrian sunlight pierce the Stygian gloom.

Wide and impressive as is no other Eastern suq that I have seen, a casual wanderer there has space to move without being jostled by donkeys, scooters, cars or trundling handcarts, as is the case in the more tortuous confines of the city. Carpet sellers, jewellers, perfume vendors, spice merchants and the purveyors of the superb dried apricots of the region, rub shoulders there nowadays with the sellers of plastic goods and mass-produced international clothing.

The Long Suq leads to Bal esh Shaqi, the Gate of the East, and the most interesting Roman relic in Damascus. Even after the impressive suq, the scale of this battered marble gateway brings one up short, strikes a chord, creates a link. It was standing here when Christ walked this earth. St Paul probably

walked through it when he was led here sightless. He had travelled to the city with the expectation of arresting scores if not
hundreds of Christ's followers and instead, for the first time,
preached in the synagogues of Damascus that this same Christ
was the Son of God.

Almost before there is time for the significance of this gate to
sink in another marvel of Damascus is in view just beyond. The
great Umayyad Mosque is undoubtedly the glory of Damascus
if not of the entire Muslim world; even in Cairo I have not seen
a greater. It began as a Byzantine church of great splendour
and, as is common in Islam, what could be re-used or adapted
was incorporated, especially the basic walls and the pillars. The
result is a triumph though so subtle a one it is difficult to say
quite why it is so. I finally decided it was primarily the proportions of the main hall which are extraordinarily long and
slender, making it seem prayerful and exciting at one and the
same time. The fame and splendour of the Umayyad Mosque,
however, lie in the courtyard where huge expanses of mosaics in
marvellous greens and gold emblazon huge surfaces of wall.
Probably the work of Byzantine craftsmen they seem to bridge
the divide between Islam and Christianity, especially in one vast
work which looks for all the world like the Tree of Life.

Beyond the bulk of the Umayyad Mosque the Street called
Straight is narrow and less dramatic. Not difficult I felt to
imagine the world of the Early Church here where the various
churches of today's Syrian Christian community rub shoulders
with shops, workshops and mosques. Down one side street can
be found the house of Ananias who restored Paul's sight, now a
regular maintained monument of the city.

I came there a half-hour before it was due to open and sat on
a stone nearby to wait and write up my notes. But I had time to
record only a few words before a man was insisting that I come
and wait more comfortably in his house which was close by. No
sooner was I seated there in a pleasant upstairs sitting-room
than the man's brother appeared with a take-away meal of
chicken, bread, pickle and cheese, and I was pressed to eat with
them. Deftly, with fingers and pitta bread instead of cutlery the
meal was consumed; one more eucharist on the journey.

I had seen the house of Ananias before, as well as the place where St Paul is said to have been let down over the walls in a basket to escape the wrath of the Jews. But the little chapel at the level of the Roman city which is about twelve feet below the present day pavement does not pall. The rough cut stone of the walls, the shaft of dusty light from the domed roof are all authentic Roman stuff of the right period. Moreover, as in the Holy City itself, the living tradition of the believing community kept the tradition of such places alive, even when they were buried beneath rubble or, in the case of Ananias's house, made into a mosque. In such places to touch the fabric is to feel the years recede.

There was a tenderness in Damascus which I had not felt there before, so perhaps it was some change in me. Reaching sixty has some distinct advantages in Arab lands, not the least of which is being treated with respect, which in turn allows me to be more relaxed and less on my guard. Last time I was in Syria the main problem was avoiding having my bottom pinched by silly young men; ten years clearly makes a difference. Now I could accept invitations to drink tea or coffee, to see interesting objects or take pictures from people's balconies without worrying about hidden motives.

Everyone, except a surly official in the Umayyad Mosque, seemed to be friendly to me in Damascus, but it was with some young carpet sellers that I developed the closest rapport in the three short days I spent there. One store, where a young man called Ismael worked, had some of the finest old carpets I had ever been allowed to examine closely. Many were in holes, and Ismael and his father specialized in repairing them, matching the thread by colour, weight and age and using the same techniques of weaving as in the original, so that the end result was virtually indistinguishable. When they gave me their card I protested at the word 'darning' used to describe this skilful work, and suggested they substitute 'restored' or 'restoration'. From there it was but a step for them to take me to their printer so we could plan out a new card together with no errors of grammar. After that I would not have been allowed to pass without stopping for a chat and a glass of tea. In another small carpet store a young man called Ahmed was studying English, and on the first occasion we met he lent me some of his books, trusting absolutely that I would return them as promised.

From both young men I gained some first-hand idea of the economic and social changes taking place in their country. The most obvious ones for them were the gradual emancipation of women (something they claimed they fully approved of since it gave them far more contact with the opposite sex), a change to a more Western scale of values, and the continuing fight against poverty as ambitions grew and standards altered. Both men had aspirations of a different life style; Ahmed would like to go to America to study English literature. Ismael wanted to be an accountant. Nonetheless, both were proud of their traditional inherited skills even though they felt the security it offered them was minimal now, and not something they would be likely to pass on to their own sons. We discussed these things slowly, an idea or two at a time over tiny cups of coffee or glasses of tea. Sometimes friends or customers dropped in and added their ideas and thoughts to the conversation.

Ten years previously the main frustrations I had heard voiced in Syria had all been to do with Israel and what was felt to be her expansionist policies. Having seized and held on to the Golan Heights, the 'security zone' in Lebanon, and all of the West Bank and Gaza many Syrians feared that, with American backing, Israel would stop at nothing until the whole of Greater Syria was under her control, fears that had been fanned by both America's and Israel's involvement in the politics of other Arab countries, particularly Iran and Iraq. It touched on a raw nerve in the Arab sense of rightness and justice. It was not fair. In a straight fight against Israel they felt they had a good chance, but with America pouring in money and armaments it was like fighting a monstrous Hydra, whose heads always regrew no matter how often they were severed.

I heard no such sentiments expressed this time. Perhaps Syria's role as peacekeeper in the Lebanon war had resulted in a new sense of national worth and responsibility. And perhaps the country's growing prosperity turned aspirations to more prosaic concerns. On the question of the present Middle East peace moves most Syrians seemed to think their country was in a strong position, both morally and politically. 'Give us back our Golan and then we will talk about peace,' was President Assad's strongly-voiced position, and the whole country seemed to be solidly behind him in this.

President Assad has been in power for a long time now. He has won his major internal battles with extreme Islamic militants and his regime seems to have mellowed somewhat. Whether that regime is regarded as an out-and-out dictatorship, or as something closer to benign paternalism, there is certainly some virtue in a strong stable leadership, especially in this part of the world. There is a tendency in the West to condemn out of hand any form of government that is not a democracy. Though what we consider a 'democracy' to be has many shades of meaning and is, I suggest, no guarantee of individual freedom, national security or economic prosperity. The sickly Ottoman Empire left a terrible legacy of corruption, mismanagement and poverty to the entire region, and fifty years of self rule is a very short time to undo all those centuries of damage.

The countries of the Middle East came into existence within their present boundaries only after World War One, when the Ottoman Empire collapsed. Britain and France literally drew the map of the Middle East with pencils and rulers. Not unnaturally, in what was essentially a tribal society, there were many different contenders for these 'new' countries; countless conflicting claims and counter-claims. The immediate need was for stability. Only when a strong man succeeded in gaining power and holding on to it did a country move forward, as in Syria.

Lebanon tried a system of democracy with all sorts of built in safeguards – some posts could be filled only by Muslims, some by Christians, some by the Druse and so forth. The West considered it the best and most stable regime in the area. Yet under the first real pressure it destabilized into the bloodiest of civil wars.

The first time I visited Syria I was very aware of the presence of secret police and the armies of paid informers. The iron fist of control was obvious everywhere, as were the strong under-currents of hostility towards the President and his regime. I spent only a short time in the country on this occasion but the atmosphere was noticeably different. There were probably still informers and secret police about, but they were certainly keeping a lower profile. People in the street were altogether freer and more spontaneous. There was not the perpetual looking over the shoulder that I remembered. Also no one, including my friends of the suq, spoke in terms other than of respect for their ageing president. It might have been a grudging respect from some of them, but it was not fear. A great regret was expressed that Assad's son, who had died recently, would not now be taking over the reins of government from him. If there was fear it was on that score. They knew what they had in President Assad, but what would follow?

At which point a silence would descend over our little gathering until someone changed the subject or snapped his fingers to send a boy running for another round of tea.

Apart from the Christian brothers who had fed me near the house of Ananias all the acquaintances I made in Damascus were Muslims. Yet the feeling of being at home and happy there was in no way different to what I had felt among the Christian Armenians of Lebanon. When the day of departure dawned, it proved just as hard to tear myself away from Damascus and continue the journey towards Jerusalem.

CHAPTER SIX

South into Jordan

Travellers and pilgrims could once go directly to Jerusalem from Damascus, retracing the footsteps of St Paul. There is a choice of two traditional, time-honoured routes between the cities. One goes south, and descending ever deeper below sea level into the trough of the Jordan Valley brings the traveller to the waving palms of Jericho before turning to the west for the crossing of the Jordan and the long steep climb up to Jerusalem. But this is a hot and humid route, especially in summer. The more favoured way and the one most likely to have been followed by St Paul, hugs the skirts of the Lebanon Mountains and crosses the River Jordan at the ford of Jisr Banat Ya'coub, the 'Ford of the Daughters of Jacob'. This road comes down through Galilee and leads eventually to the Damascus Gate on the east side of the Holy City.

For Christians there is a tremendous sense of drama in this approach to what was the setting of so much of the life and teaching of Jesus. When the journey is on foot or by bicycle this is especially so as the events unfold slowly enough to make their mark. The road winds around the southern slopes of Mount Hermon and as it begins its descent to the plains of Galilee, a small round lake ringed by green hills comes into view below. Such is the distance that little of the overlay of the twentieth century intrudes upon the scene. When I first travelled that way, although I knew I would come to the Sea of Galilee at some point, I was quite unprepared for the impact it made lying there in its entirety below me. The realization that it was on the near shore of this actual body of water that the Risen Christ had once made breakfast for his disciples in the grey light of a troubled dawn has remained for me one of the foremost experiences of my travels.

It was probably the cold grey mist of the present dawn that made me remember that first sight of the Sea of Galilee as I headed due south out of Damascus, making for Dera'a and the Jordan border by a far less scenic route. I had to go this way if I was to take up the invitation to see for myself what the Jordanian Peace meant. But in any case I had no choice of routes. Modern politics have closed most of the ancient highways of the Holy Land. There is now no easy way of getting into Israel except by flying there direct or coming by boat to Haifa. Israel welcomes tourists, especially ones who stay in expensive hotels and swell the country's economy, but is not at all keen on travellers who want to stray from the usual paths, or on writers who ask awkward questions.

When I was planning my first pilgrimage from London to Jerusalem ten years before, I had been warned that Israel would not allow my bicycle entry. I could fly it in direct, no problem, but I could not ride it in overland, not even if I was prepared to take it to pieces myself at the border to prove that it was not stuffed with explosives. I could not even bring it in by the buses that took tourists to and fro from Jordan. I asked the British Foreign Office what I should do, since a bicycle journey to Jerusalem could hardly stop on the wrong side of the Jordan. The Foreign Office, who said they could think of no less likely scenario than that of a middle-aged female writer bicycling four thousand and odd miles just to blow up the Allenby Bridge (which was built by the British anyway), kindly offered to arrange the matter at diplomatic level, well in advance. This they did and a few days before I was due to cross, the British Embassy in Amman telexed the Israeli authorities to remind them of the agreement, and to give them the exact date and time I would arrive at the border.

It should all have been plain sailing. But in fact when I arrived at the crossing I was refused permission to enter, and the big guns were kept trained on me for the six hours I stuck it out there, sitting in no man's land in the heat and dust, refusing to go back into Jordan but not allowed forward into the West Bank.

The impasse ended eventually because the bus loads of

tourists who were crossing in both directions began to express their puzzlement and concern that a harmless-looking middle-aged cyclist was being subjected to this heavy-handed harassment. Afterwards when I wrote up the incident, Jewish newspapers in many countries expressed amazement that Israel, to whom they gave such generous support, should prove so lacking in public relations.

There was a rumour that control had been relaxed a little now with the Jordanian/Israeli Peace, and that there was even an additional crossing open to travellers, down by the Red Sea. No one had been able to confirm this in the Israeli Tourist Office in London, however, so I gathered the situation was still fluid. I would need to make enquiries when I got to Amman.

The weather had been very cold at night in Damascus though the days were bright and sunny. But today, as I worked my way through the bleak southern suburbs of the city, an expanding area of building sites and raw, ugly housing blocks, a grey mist kept visibility down to a hundred yards or so. It was the morning rush hour and men with scarves wrapped around their heads lined the verges waiting for buses that swooped and swerved like swallows, cutting across the bows of any other road user including cyclists. It needed skill to stay alive and I had little time to watch the view. No hardship this, for mile after mile the prospect was unrelieved except where the housing thinned to give glimpses of winter fields smothered under a dusting of urban litter.

Once I had left the industrial environs of Damascus and had time to think of things other than brute survival I realized how chill it was. It was like the rawest day of an English winter and although I was wearing all my layers of clothing, including my Gore-tex jacket and over-trousers, only very brisk pedalling was keeping my blood from freezing. Imitating the Damascus workers I stopped to wrap a scarf around my head, remembering ruefully the warm hat left in the taxi on Cyprus. Fortunately I had a second pair of gloves so I did not need to use socks or plastic bags to protect my hands.

Only slowly did I come to realize that the seemingly awful day was redeemed by a splendid wind blowing fiercely from the north. Bicyclists are very sensitive to adverse winds, but we often don't notice when they are in our favour, helping to push us along. We are all too ready to assume that the unaccustomed speed and ease of our progress is the result of suddenly finding our true cycling form. This desert wind, however, was too strong to be ignored, and once I was aware of its force I stopped to make adjustments to my handlebars, so that I could sit bolt upright and present the greatest possible area to its helpful force.

Strangely enough, although the wind continued to blow strongly, the mist did not lift for some hours. I careered along, sailing rather than cycling, devouring the miles but seeing nothing beyond fifty or so yards on either side of me. These margins of rich-brown newly-ploughed fields were punctuated occasionally by patches of grassy meadow so intensely green as to seem unreal.

Bands of semi-feral dogs would appear suddenly out of the mist, setting my heart racing as they tore along at full stretch on a converging course. But even as I reached for my Dog Dazer – a device I always keep ready to hand to repel such attacks – the dogs were already slowing and falling back, so fast was my wind-assisted progress.

I discovered later that I was not on the road I had intended travelling. Signs had directed me onto one that had been built only recently. The old road stringing together the villages which I had previously cycled twelve years before was away on my right. Apart from the dogs and a very occasional truck or car, this new highway was empty and I saw no living person and scarcely a building for practically the entire seventy miles. It was like journeying through a ghost country – not an unnatural reaction, for strangely enough the road roughly followed the Via Nova Traiana, the great Roman highway of the East that marched over three hundred miles through Greater Syria joining the colonial towns and settlements.

Only as I neared Dera'a and came to a signpost pointing to Bosra was I back in a world I remembered. Bosra is a splendid place, one of the Graeco-Roman towns served by the Nova Traiana, and very individual due to its being built out of the basalt rock of the region. I had found it wonderfully strange to see soaring fluted Greek columns that were pitch black instead of the usual white marble. Being off the beaten track of later civilizations Bosra has managed to preserve many wonderful fragments of its past and is full of atmosphere. It was for a while an important stop on the pilgrim road to Mecca and even boasted a footprint of Muhammad's horse which had been miraculously imprinted in the stone floor of a mosque.

The city's chief claim to fame, however, is a Roman theatre in almost pristine condition, because in the late seventh century it was incorporated snugly into a strong Muslim citadel. The fortress proved most satisfactory against the marauding bands who preyed on the large pilgrim convoys, but it really came into its own during the Crusades. Three times Crusader armies marched on Bosra and each time retired without exchanging blows.

Having once spent a very happy day among the monuments, entertained by a charming Syrian family, I was sorely tempted to go back there now, and I stopped undecided at the cross-roads while some local people tried to help by saying 'Bosra, Bosra' and pointing in that direction. But time was short, and reluctantly I turned in the opposite direction and headed for Dera'a and the border.

Dera'a also boasts a proud history but unlike Bosra not a jot of it has survived in any tangible state. Modern Dera'a could beat most unlovely towns for crumbling concrete, water-logged broken roads and pavements and an atmosphere of hopeless inertia. It also suffers from an endless stream of lorries trundling through to the border. I had no choice but to stay there since there was no other town for miles. Two hotels, both equally squalid, and neither with any form of heating, offered the only shelter. I went through a parody of bargaining for a room in what might have been the better of the two, and the fierce little hotelier, who was sensibly wrapped in two sheepskin coats, won hands down. As he waved his arms about, extolling the virtues of the dank little cell he was offering me, our breath condensed before us in awesome clouds. I assented to his price quickly in order to escape outside where it was considerably warmer.

Yet even in Dera'a there was warmth and hospitality to be found. The hotelier himself invited me into his office where a stove took the chill off the air and kept a kettle bubbling for the endless glasses of tea that clearly punctuated his day. Two other guests, a father and son, were also being entertained. The son who was no more than fifteen, tall and slender and very handsome in his white gelabiyeh and Arab headdress, kept his eyes fixed on his shoes, and seemed to be in an agony of embarrassment.

Wandering the streets afterwards, since it was too cold to remain in the hotel, I found a shop where I could spend the remains of my Syrian currency on bread and cheese and fruit. The young man behind the counter was, he told me, a part-time student and eager to practise his English. Getting a younger friend to mind his shop he walked me around the corner home to meet his family – mother, father and six younger siblings. Their first-floor apartment appeared very spacious because it had little furniture apart from the television. Everyone was sitting on the floor on a carpet around a low round table. The father spoke English reasonably well and apparently held down a good job in local administration, but even so, he said, he could not earn enough to meet all the family needs, especially in education. None of his sons would enjoy the benefits he himself had enjoyed, which was sad.

The meal to which the son had invited me did not seem adequate for so many, and since his parents had not been expecting me I was able to decline on the pretext of having already eaten. The blissful warmth of the apartment was hospitality enough for me.

I asked the father what he thought about the current peace moves in the Middle East. His response was to talk at length about the historical hatred between Jews and Arabs, which would, he thought, prevent any real peace between them. This present business was just playing for time on Israel's part. Syria, he said, was fortunate in having a strong leader and no pressing need to do anything. It was far more difficult for Jordan who was directly involved. Only when the Arab nations had achieved a true economic stability would the Middle East be in any position to talk real peace, and that time would certainly herald the end of the State of Israel, since co-existence was not possible. Until then, the Arab nations just had to put up with Israel's bullying. On which gloomy note I took my leave.

Having exhausted the possibilities of Dera'a I returned to the hotel and snuggled down in my full camping gear – down sleeping bag lined with a warm silk inner bag, and a waterproof Gore-tex bivvy bag as an outer cover. Under me, to further offset the damp bedding, was my inflatable camping mattress. The only advantages the room offered above sleeping under the stars appeared to be the bright, naked light bulb and the dubious plumbing – hot water was not one of the hotel's amenities. My supper of bread and cheese did not require me to leave my cocoon; I could even light the stove and make a hot cup of tea without rising. By nine o'clock I was asleep; seventy miles even with the wind behind one is quite a stretch. As yet I had not put in the successive days of riding that lead to fitness, nor would this journey provide such opportunities.

In the morning I lit my stove again to make coffee before even thinking of emerging from my layers. There was a film of moisture on the top of the bivvy bag, and my breath hung thickly in the frigid air. It was a pleasant surprise therefore to emerge from the unlovely environs of the hotel into a much warmer day, with the sun just breaking through thinning cloud.

With so many lorries and trucks pouring across the Syrian border I felt myself fortunate to be processed with a minimum of fuss. The Jordanian crossing was almost as easy, the only problem there was unfamiliarity with the bicycle as a means of international transport. The Jordanian customs official was above chalking a bicycle's panniers with his formal squiggle, while the soldier at the exit gate would not let me through without this seal of approval. All of which caused some unnecessary to-ing and fro-ing until, after a few abortive trips I complained to the officer in charge and was given the services of a soldier to clear the way for me.

As in life generally, so in travel, nothing is ever quite perfect.

The weather was now like a warm summer's day in England. With a good road under my wheels I was riding through the biblical lands of Gilead through scenery which grew ever more attractive. But with the departure of the cloud and mist the wind had also changed and now blew with equal force from the opposite direction, turning the ride into a struggle. The road ran along the line of the Graeco-Roman cities of the Decapolis, the most splendidly preserved of which, Jerash, lay directly on my route and I planned to spend the night there after exploring the ruins.

By the time I came to the turning for Jerash, the combined effects of the hills of Gilead and the adverse wind had taken their toll. I felt exhausted. From primitive terraced villages high above the road women called out to me, inviting me by signs to come and drink tea with them. Much as I was tempted, I hadn't the energy to scramble up those precipitous paths. I was also feeling the effects of having eaten only sparingly for the past two days and knew that I should press on to Jerash and find a substantial meal. But the road ran on; the sun grew ever hotter and the way steeper. As I toiled on foot up the final slopes I was in shirt-sleeves and panting for a drink of water.

My arrival at the summit coincided with that of a small local bus. One of the two young men who alighted from it at once spotted the empty water bottle I was holding and went into a nearby house to get it filled. When he returned he was accompanied by three women, two of whom had young children clutching at their skirts and peeping shyly out at me from the folds. The older woman took my arm and gestured for me to accompany her. She led me onto the flat roof of her house which was more or less on a level with the road – all the rooms of the house were below, on several levels, built flat up against the precipitous hillside. This was the rim of the wide, fertile bowl that cradles Jerash, and seeing its richness spread out before me I could well believe that the great wealth of the city had been founded on agriculture.

There was no time to look around just then, however, for the lovely ritual of Bedouin hospitality was immediately in full spate. The matriarch gave orders and her two daughters hurried to do her bidding while the children looked on shyly, ready to bolt if the stranger should make a move in their direction. Cushions and rugs were spread for me to sit on, a tray was set beside me, laden with flat bread and dishes of olives and cheese, and I was bidden to eat. Water was brought, then tea, and when it was clear that I could eat and drink no more, very small cups of delicious Arabic coffee were served to the matriarch and myself. As a final gesture of hospitality a kitchen chair was brought out, in case I should prefer that to the cushions.

My knowledge of the Arabic language is limited to about a couple of dozen basic words like 'bread' and 'water', with a few added grace notes such as 'please', 'thank you' and 'I greet you in the name of Allah'. But even with this pathetic amount, the matriarch and I managed to achieve quite a reasonable level of communication. We established that we were both grand-mothers, and which children sprawling around the roof belonged to which daughter and what they were all called and, most importantly, that we were both admirers of King Hussein (she brought out a framed photograph of him to show me). My greatest triumph in her eyes was that I thought her olives the best I had ever tasted, and had no problem in conveying this fact to her. So pleased was she that she insisted on packing up a large plastic bag of them for me to take with me when I left, though in fact I was urged not to go at all but to spend the night there with them. All of which just goes to show that what we call communication is often simply a matter of one heart speaking to another with a word and a gesture here and there to illustrate a point. On parting I gave her the gas lighter which I used for the stove. It was the only thing I could think of, but I feel sure she received it as the token of friendship I intended it to be.

Fortified and relaxed I cycled on the short distance to Jerash, where the impact of the sheer extent and majesty of the ruins was such that I decided I must have been blind when I first saw them ten years earlier. I remember being impressed by them, but not totally bowled over as I was on this occasion. A lot more restoration work had been done it is true, but the biggest difference probably was that this time it was winter and I had the site almost to myself, and also perhaps, the intervening ten years had made me better able to appreciate them.

The sun remained unclouded and with the fresh breeze keeping it cool, a better day for exploring ruins could not be imagined. I left Roberts with the tourist police and gave myself up to an afternoon of pure pleasure.

For all the centuries that Jerash lay in ruins, a broken wilderness of pits and mounds of rubble, the city was a byword for destroyed magnificence, its name synonymous with desolation.

Cleared and excavated, with many of its walls and gates and columns raised, its theatres rebuilt and the great colonnaded main thoroughfare, the Cardo Maximus, revealed with its original limestone slabs rutted by chariot wheels, it is magnificent. It also offers a significant insight into the Roman world into which Jesus was born. Jesus himself probably never saw Jerash; in the three years or so of his ministry he seems not to have travelled any distance beyond Galilee and the environs of Jerusalem. But many of his disciples would have come here, and some would have preached the gospel within its walls.

What Jerash reveals so well is the absolute power of Rome; it is impossible to imagine any other civilization producing it. Here on the edge of the Empire is not a mere provincial town, but a city that in its display of enormous power and wealth, technical skill and administrative genius magnificently personifies Rome's ideals of excellence. Without the Pax Romana there could have been no Jerash. It made me realize that the Roman Empire did not simply set out to conquer new territory and exploit the natural wealth there. Nor was trade necessarily the first consideration. The real object was to turn the wider world into Rome. No matter what sacrifices Romans offered up at their many and various altars, Rome itself was really their one true god. So unquestionably superior in Roman eyes was the Graeco-Roman civilization, that they believed any tribe or country coming under their law should count itself fortunate.

Rome of course was not alone in holding such notions of superiority; other empires and would-be world dominators have cherished similar views, but none have achieved their goal as absolutely as did Rome. The obverse side of the Pax Romana was of course the iron fist of Rome maintaining its rule over its subject nations through agonizing executions and repressive legislation. But most of the powers Rome replaced were equally cruel. To have been a slave in Roman times was probably no worse than being a slave under any other power, and possibly better than under some. But one of the good things about the Roman Empire was that it was not exclusive; it was not a closed society. Given luck or ability – preferably both – individuals of subject nations could achieve Roman citizenship. And it is interesting to remember that St Paul was proud of his, as well as finding it tremendously useful to his great work.

Five hours of wandering about the gracious ruins of Jerash, of craning my neck to gaze upwards along the immense and lovely shafts of Ionic and Corinthian columns, of sitting in the two theatres (with numbered seating for wealthier Romans to reserve their places), took me back through the centuries. I became quite converted to the idea of being a provincial Roman in the heyday of the Empire, walking and disputing in the elegant oval forum and climbing the lovely flights of steps to the great temple of Artemis. I was less keen on the idea of being a Christian there in the Byzantine period, when the lovely pagan temples were hacked about to provide building material for inferior Christian basilicas. For by that time Jerash was in decline, losing its glory, a fate shared by most of the civilized world. Once the Pax Romana began to wither at its edges under the onslaught of the Turkic tribes of Central Asia it was only a matter of time before Rome itself would fall. But even under the Ottomans this part of the Empire has yet to achieve a period of peace as long as that which Rome itself imposed.

But it was the hope of a new peace which had brought me here I remembered, as I sat lost in my historical imaginings, the natural outcome of ruin visiting. Nothing could have seemed more peaceful than Jerash on this sunny day. Local men and boys used the ruins as an extension of their villages which were all around the perimeter wall. They played ball games in the open spaces and sat talking with their friends in the forum and the theatres and strolled along the Cardo Maximus on their way home. In the summer they told me it was different, then they were busy selling 'antiquities' to the tourists.

I had planned to stay in Jerash for the night and go on to Amman in the morning, but when I returned to the tourist police post to collect Roberts I found the police had other plans for me. They took their jobs very seriously; the safety of tourists was their chief concern. It was not safe for a woman to be on her own and it would soon grow dark. I must stay there where they could protect me.

Fifteen years of travelling in some of the most male-dominated parts of the world have made me neither more, nor less of a feminist. I don't in the least mind men thinking they must protect me, as long as they don't try to restrain me by force. I had to stay somewhere, and if they were prepared to make me up a bed on the floor of the half-built rest house I was not going to rebuff their good intentions. It meant one more night of not being able to wash off the sweat and dust of the day, since the sanitary arrangements were as yet barely rudimentary. On the plus side I had a room to myself, forty feet long with enough neon lights to illuminate a sizeable shopping arcade. I had to share it with some picks and shovels and a few hundred-weight of assorted rubble, but there was room enough and a door I could shut and lock.

Before it was quite dark I made my way down to the nearest signs of life, a bus flanked by a few sandwich stalls. Fruit and a flat pitta bread stuffed with cold fried felafel was all that was available; but I remembered that in my bags were the splendid olives which would add a bit of zest. Having bought my supper I headed back with a small boy escorting me politely up the steep steps and trying to tempt me to transfer my base to a room in his mother's house. Failing that he asked equally politely for money, and finally departed with a little skip of pleasure, clutching the biro I had given him.

CHAPTER SEVEN

A Temporary Shift
into Luxury

After basking in the expansive magnificence of Jerash, Amman, the capital of Jordan, comes as a shock. From the very dawn of history, and long before it became another proud city of the Decapolis known as Philadelphia, it had seen the turbulent tides of Middle Eastern history sweep around it. Its present name derives from Old Testament times when it was Rabbath-Ammon, the centre of the Ammonite kingdom. But all save a token fragment of this long human drama lies buried under the vast and featureless concrete shroud of the modern city. Even the dramatic site of Amman on its seven steep hills does little to relieve the monotony of the uninspired hard-edged architecture. The close-packed white streets, glaring fiercely under clear desert skies march over every prospect, throwing back the heat, the noise and the fumes of endless horn-blaring traffic.

I arrived there once again feeling fairly shattered after the ride from Jerash. The distance itself is no more than forty miles and the way is pleasant, winding as it does through a pleasant pastoral landscape of ochre-coloured hills, terraced and planted with olive groves. Clusters of simple clay brick cabins that blend into the landscape and flocks of dusty sheep following after their shepherds add a biblical flavour. But the switch-back road having finished with the hills of Gideon presented longer and steeper gradients once it entered the territory of the ancient Ammonites. To add to the difficulties my over-laden bicycle developed gear trouble and the chain kept jumping from cog to cog, dissipating my efforts when the need was greatest.

At one point when I was grinding my way slowly up a long

ascent a young man was able to dash out and pinch my bottom. Another time I might have dismissed such a senseless incident with a shrug, but I suppose the heat and the effort had made me irritable for I turned and gave chase, narrowly avoiding oncoming traffic. It was certainly unchristian and doubtless undignified too, but I have to admit it was also very satisfying to land a retaliatory clip on the offender's ear as he ran off laughing.

A coffee seller plying his wares by the roadside, who had witnessed the entire scene, hurried over with a complimentary drink and apologies for the behaviour of his fellow countryman. No real Jordanian would have done such a thing, he said, he must be a refugee, unhinged by the troubles of his life, and probably with no father to put him right. It was good I had taught him a lesson.

I was not so sure about the last sentiment, but the coffee vendor's remarks served as a reminder of the extraordinary demographic nature of the country I was now in. Thinking about it as I rode on, I remembered how perplexed I had been on my first visit to Jordan. It had seemed impossible then to know who was Jordanian and who Palestinian, especially as many people claimed there was no difference anyway. It was reckoned that as much as a third of Jordan's population was Palestinian, and clearly there was a difference, since that third consisted almost entirely of displaced people.

In 1948, when the State of Israel came into existence, tens of thousands of Palestinians fled across the border into Jordan in fear of their lives, a panic deliberately orchestrated by the Israelis with the aid of a couple of well-publicized massacres. Many Palestinians intended only to place their families in safety before returning immediately to protect their houses and property. But the houses, and in some cases whole villages, of those who fled were immediately seized by Israel and never returned to their rightful owners. There were also many cases of Palestinians who refused to be pressured or terrorized into fleeing, and who were forcibly expelled from their homes at gunpoint.

Another massive exodus of Palestinians occurred after the Six Day War in 1967, a war which put an effective end to the Jordanian administration of the West Bank. Israel was now in control of all the remaining land of the Palestinians, both in the West Bank and Gaza, and in spite of international censure, administered the areas as an army of occupation.

A policy of confiscating strategic pockets of Palestinian land in the occupied territories began immediately. At first this expropriated land was claimed to be for military use, but after lying idle for a year or so it was turned over to the civil authorities for the building of Israeli settlements. The dispossessed Palestinians in the meantime had swelled the numbers of Jordan's population.

The incoming Jewish settlers, many from America, knew little if anything of the complicated history of the country they were coming to, or of the wider world of the Middle East, and nothing at all about the actual parcel of land they were taking over. All they saw was the derelict state of it, untended as it had been since the Palestinians were turned off it. The settlers added fuel to the bitterness of the dispossessed Palestinian farmers by voicing such sentiments as: 'This land belonged to nobody; it was lying idle. If the Arabs had cared about it they would have worked it.' In spite of the centuries of careful Arab husbandry, the beautifully built and carefully maintained terracing of the hillsides, Israeli propaganda took root – 'Arabs don't care about their land.' Nothing could be further from the truth.

As Israeli harassment was stepped up by punitive legislation, by curfews and by other mass punishments, by administrative arrests and imprisonment, and by further wholesale seizure of land for Israeli settlements in the West Bank and Gaza, more and more Palestinians found themselves with little choice but to leave for Jordan.

At that time too, Palestinians studying abroad, as well as those who for any reason at all were out of the country, were not allowed back into Israel. A desperately cruel embargo this, for it split hundreds of families and is still in force today. All these thousands of displaced Palestinians have swelled Jordan's population, often in sudden huge numbers, a situation difficult for any economy to manage, but particularly so for one of the poorest countries in the Middle East.

Only those Palestinians who were entirely destitute and who ended up in camps were officially registered by international agencies as refugees. Palestinians who could maintain themselves and their families in Jordan, or who could find work in other countries were not counted, so the total number of the dispossessed can never be known.

The situation created endless problems for Jordan, not least of which was the presence of the Palestinian Liberation Organization on Jordanian soil. In spite of the deep sympathy King Hussein and his people undoubtedly felt for the Palestinian cause, militant action by the PLO to attract world attention to their plight was deeply embarrassing to Jordan's position with the West. It also attracted punitive retaliatory raids from Israel. Matters came to a head in September 1970 when three hijacked Western airliners were landed at a disused airfield in the east of the country.

Jordan's solution was to get rid of the PLO without warning in a sudden and concerted action. It was not a particularly savoury episode. Many Palestinian lives were lost unnecessarily, and deep and lasting bitterness resulted from it. To the Arab world at large it seemed a betrayal and earned Jordan a great deal of criticism. It also caused such despair and frustration among Palestinians that the notorious 'Black September' movement was formed. This undisciplined group of militant extremists, feeling they now had nothing left to lose, engaged in a series of violent terrorist acts, including the killing of nine Israeli athletes they had taken hostage at the Munich Olympic Games. None of which, of course, did anything to foster world sympathy for the Palestinian cause.

With the expulsion of the last of the Palestinian guerillas in 1971 Jordan's threatened stability was restored and the punitive Israeli reprisal attacks were now turned upon poor Lebanon, Israel's other unfortunate neighbour.

Having so recently come from Lebanon and seen with my own eyes something of what it means to be the unwilling hosts of a guerilla force, I found myself far more in sympathy with

Jordan's dilemma. By expelling the PLO at least the country survived intact, without civil war and without the direct interference of foreign powers, all of which spells no small victory in this part of the world. And now, seemingly, against all the odds, there was a peace treaty in force with Jordan's former bitter enemy.

Understanding a little more about the country and its problems was making, I realized, a great difference to this journey. The understanding had come about slowly, through reading and discussions over the past years, and more lately through my meeting with King Hussein. Ten years before I had possessed neither the knowledge of the complicated political issues nor the essential unbiased openness to understand what I was seeing. I had held the common Western view that Israel was essentially right and to be admired for her courage and firmness, while the Arab world was the aggressor and almost entirely in the wrong. I had travelled fairly widely through the country at that time, and had enjoyed friendly contacts with individual Jordanians, but my sympathies had not been engaged in the way they now were. Being somewhat better informed, I also found I was enjoying myself far more.

My feelings towards Amman, however, had not changed in the least; it still struck me as the most unattractive and boring of cities. It is so big and amorphous as to suggest that the entire population of Jordan has been swallowed in its maw, which indeed is not so far from the truth. Since most of Jordan is desert, and much of the arable land is unproductive because of the chronic water shortage, a disproportionate number of Jordanians do live in the capital. Just as on the previous visit, faced with the featureless urban sprawl in which I despaired of finding my way, I was reminded of the Minotaur's maze, and feared there would prove to be no way out. Not one single landmark had made enough impression on me to be remembered.

Taking the line of least resistance, I simply freewheeled down and down and down until I found myself in the appropriately named Downtown Amman which at least is recognizably different from the rest of the city. Here on one of the few level places lie the token vestiges of Imperial Rome, together with the worst noise, the densest traffic and the thickest dust of the entire city. The sense of being caught in the centre of the maze tightened my incipient claustrophobia several notches, and in spite of my fatigue I rapidly retraced my way uphill.

I booked into the first hotel that would have me, and found it was essentially a place in which elderly ex-Palestinian activists gathered when visiting Amman. Later that evening I talked to some of them over glasses of tea and found them a challenging if rather cynical company. Many had spent time in Israeli prisons and all were deeply sceptical about the present peace moves. Although I felt shy of putting my questions to such men for fear they would think me naïve, I was answered seriously and several useful introductions resulted from the meeting.

The hotel had an air of faded middle-class gentility, which is to say the carpets became more frayed the higher up one went. At my own request I was given a room on the top floor, so as to be as far as possible from the traffic noise. At this level the carpets were in actual holes, but the room was clean enough and reasonably comfortable, supplied with the standard equipment of fan, refrigerator and television, none of which I needed. After the hard ride I looked forward only to an uninterrupted night's sleep. That, however, was not forthcoming as the following brief and despairing entry in my journal records.

2 a.m. Tired to death but sleep impossible. Sodom and Gomorrah could not have been worse than this city!

Overstated perhaps, but I do find noise pollution one of the worst forms of torture, and Amman has more than its fair share of it. The problem is the plethora of streets which are separated only by very narrow bands of land on which the buildings stand. One road ran right up against the back of the hotel and another hugged the front with the narrowest of pavements between. Being sandwiched between these two rushing streams of ceaseless traffic with their blazing lights and insistent, cacophonous horns was not a happy experience.

Dawn found me still sleepless and very wan. I was fully resolved to leave Amman immediately if I failed to make contact with the people who were supposed to be helping me gather the information I had come to seek. Roughing it is one thing. A night like the one at Jerash camped on the floor of a building site I can accept as part of the rich tapestry of travel, but a second night of this continuous battering did not bear thinking about.

Succour, however, was at hand. One telephone call and I was instructed to remove myself immediately to the Inter-Continental Hotel where I was expected and where the business of my visit could begin.

'Very expensive,' said the friendly desk clerk when I told him where I was going as I checked out. 'It is the best hotel in Amman.' And he gave me a hard look from under his eyebrows as though he thought I was swinging a line. This made me wonder if my appearance was simply not up to such elevated lodgings. I had thought I was looking my most respectable, having taken the opportunity of doing my laundry the previous evening. But such niceties are only relative. My lightweight, non-iron shirt and trousers were perfectly acceptable on the bicycle, but off it, and in the wrong surroundings, I suppose I might look a touch eccentric. All I could do to try and improve my image was to add my Gore-tex jacket to the ensemble; that at least had been a costly garment when I bought it, even if it had since assumed a travel-worn patina.

Rather overdressed for the warm morning sunshine I ped-alled off into Amman's morning traffic. I did not see one other cyclist the whole time I was in Amman, which is not really surprising, for with its precipitous hills it is undoubtedly one of the least suitable bicycling cities in the world. Fortunately I had not so far to go as to seriously overheat in my jacket. Spotting the array of international flags, I was soon turning smartly into the ample forecourt of the Inter-Continental. The usual advance guard of uniformed doormen who find repelling undesirables a welcome change from opening car doors came forward wearing stern 'You must have come to the wrong place' expressions. A cyclist riding up to the front entrance was clearly off course, even one clad in a smart Gore-tex jacket. I had a brief hysterical moment imagining their expressions had I arrived in the psychedelic body-hugging lycra garments favoured by today's cycling cognoscenti. But before there could be any unpleasantness, such as being told to go round to the back door, the person who was expecting me came to the rescue and escorted me, together with Roberts, into the hotel.

No question here of a friendly bootboy carrying my cycle up to my room. The head doorman made it quite clear that it was not his intention to have a guest making a daily habit of coming and going on a bicycle. Once the panniers were removed Roberts was firmly locked in a cupboard together with other confiscated or abandoned luggage. He would be safe there until I left, I was told, when I could reclaim him if I had not lost the receipt.

'Amazing,' runs my journal, 'how much better life seems in more comfortable surroundings!' Which for someone who promotes the joys of the simple life, and of sleeping under the stars sounds suspiciously like double standards. But novelty and contrast add spice to life, and at this stage of the journey I was due for a little comfort.

Only very occasionally do I stay in really good hotels, usually at my publishers' expense when publicizing a new work. But generous though some publishers can be at times, I have never occupied as grand an apartment as I was given at the Amman Inter-Continental, where I was, I gathered, the guest of His Majesty. I was also to be provided with the services of a car and driver to whisk me off to the various interviews arranged for me by the Ministry of Information.

Of course, being treated so courteously made me feel welcome and favourably disposed towards Jordan, but that was no bad thing. My main object in being there was to try to gain an understanding of the basis for Jordan's Peace Treaty, the thinking behind it, and the hopes for the future. To do that I needed to speak with a wide range of people from ministers to students. By selecting the people they thought I should see, Jordan had the opportunity to present herself in the best

Above: The ruins of ancient Byblos in Lebanon.

Left: The Roman Gate to the Street called Straight, Damascus.

Right: The Roman theatre, Jerash.

Below: A pastoral scene in Jordan.

Bottom left: The Bedouin family in Jerash who fed me.

Bottom right: The Madaba map.

Above: Jerusalem and the Church of the Russian Gethsemane from the Church of Dominus Flevit on the Mount of Olives.

Right: A corner of the Haram esh-Sharif, Jerusalem.

Above: Orthodox Jews in front of the Wailing Wall.

Left: The Damascus Gate.

Below: The Holy Sepulchre from the Ethiopians' roof space.

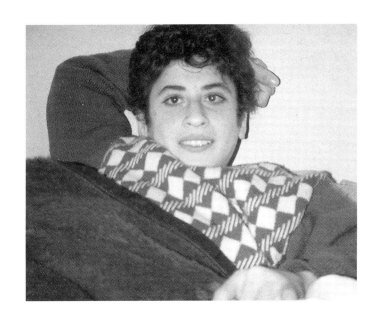

Top left: A paralysed 10-year-old boy in Gaza, shot by Israeli soldiers while placing a Palestinian flag on a roof.

Bottom left: A donkey cart with licence plate in Gaza.

Above: A procession of Armenian bishops in Jerusalem.

Right: Israeli soldiers spot check a Palestinian youth in Jerusalem.

Above: The Lion Gate.

Below: The Church of John the Baptist, the oldest church in Jerusalem.

possible light. But it was up to me to sort out the information I was given, to separate fact from wishful thinking. As I was also able to wander about freely and talk to anyone I chanced to meet, I felt there was little danger of coming away with too biased and one-sided a picture.

To balance the information gathering and to put flesh on dry facts I wanted to fit in a few visits to some of Jordan's stunning natural wonders as well as to the monuments I had not visited when I travelled there before. It was a very full schedule, and I doubt I could have done it all in the time I had available without the sort of help I was given.

So I did not in the least feel guilty about the unaccustomed luxury, I only wished there was more leisure to enjoy it to the full, especially the grand bathroom with its expansive round bath and welter of toiletries. The best of these courtesy items were the plastic shower caps which make ideal saddle covers for when a bicycle has to stand about in the rain – one of the nastier aspects of bicycling is a wet seat. As I knew I could expect abundant rain further on in my journey I collected all the plastic shower caps I was given. Since a fresh one appeared each day I had a useful store of them by the time I left.

My bedroom was on the fifth floor, and was large, light and airy. The hotel occupied a sizeable plot of land at the apex of one of Amman's hills, so the incessant roar of traffic filtered through to my Olympian heights as a distant murmur. The furnishings and decoration had a pleasant Nabbatean motif. Jordan likes to think of herself as descended from this highly individual race of ancient traders who specialized in the most eclectic composite art form of any known race. They borrowed from the styles of every culture they came up against and by combining them all produced something quite distinctive. It was the Nabbateans who carved the fabulous city of Petra out of the red sandstone rock and thus provided Jordan with its prime tourist site. So it was only fitting that Jordan's best hotel should honour the memory.

Still, I was not there to admire the decor. Within two hours of checking in I had bathed, done my laundry (my minuscule wardrobe was going to be hard pressed to live up to the surroundings), met the Minister of Information, eaten my first lunch in the hotel's large and intimidating dining room, and was heading for my first appointment in a splendid twenty-year-old Mercedes.

The driver of this staid maroon paragon with its elegant walnut-trimmed facia was Mahmoud, who was also its proud owner. His whole family, he told me, had clubbed together to help him buy it, and it would take him years to pay them all back. It was clearly the most important thing in his life, and he treated it like the crown jewels. Nonetheless at all times he drove with one arm limp and dangling from the window, his heavy gold bracelet catching the sunlight. Many other Middle Eastern drivers seem to have adopted this one-handed style of steering, and it appeared to be a point of honour never to bring the other arm inboard no matter what the circumstances. Fortunately Mahmoud was seldom in a hurry, and only very occasionally, usually in the middle of turning corners, did I find myself laying a nervous hand on the steering wheel when Mahmoud had left it unattended in order to execute a gear change.

A gangling, amiable man in his mid to late twenties, plagued by a distressing rash of pimples, Mahmoud did not in the least look like a chauffeur. He dressed with studied nonchalance in designer jeans, black rollneck sweater, leather jacket, Rolex watch and Lacoste sunglasses. He said he worked freelance, mostly for the Ministry of Information, taking Westerners like me about, and enjoyed the life very much.

Had his grasp of English been better it might have occurred to me to wonder if he was a member of Jordan's secret police. But if he was then he kept an unnaturally high profile, for he would escort me right to the desk, announcing me and my business to the receptionists, and was persuaded only with difficulty to wait in another room and not muscle in on the actual interviews.

On the other hand, one of the pleasurable things about Jordan is the sense of equality the people have. I think it probably comes from the desert inheritance, and is essentially a clan characteristic. There is nothing quite like it now in the West,

A Temporary Shift into Luxury

though I think the Highlands of Scotland enjoyed a similar spirit before Culloden and the breaking of the clans. Tremendous respect is shown for all members of the high families, particularly those who, like the King, are directly descended from the Prophet Muhammad. But mixed with the respect is also the affection of one family member for another and the right to speak on an equal footing.

I came to know Mahmoud well for I saw more of him than anyone else during the busy two weeks I spent in Jordan. When by a lucky chance, I was able to prescribe the right medicine for his duodenal ulcer (I had once suffered the same complaint) our relationship shifted a gear. He still tried to muscle in on my conversations, but he also treated me with a new respect. I was once even taken home to meet his mother.

77

CHAPTER EIGHT

A Land of Desert Idealists

What Jordan's capital city might lack in excitement is more than made up for in the wealth and variety of the desert landscapes. Small though the country is, the noble expanses of sand and rock to the south and the east of Amman confer a feeling of boundless space. It is the deserts of Jordan that attract me and I was determined to try and see a little more of them on this visit.

Deserts have always fascinated people. Places of terror into which the 'scapegoat' was once driven bearing the sins of a people, they also conferred power on those able to endure the terrifying stillness and solitude. Archetypal heroes, such as Enkidu of the Gilgamesh myth were products of the desert. Moses encountered God among the barren rocks of Sinai, and biblical prophets from Elijah to John the Baptist wrested their strength from a desert experience. Christ himself spent forty days in the wilderness.

In our over-pressured, media-dominated, speed-shrunken planet, where even the quietest of country places echo to the roar of aeroplanes, motor traffic, radios, and the chatter and whine of endless mechanical aids that are meant to enhance the quality of life, the value of space and silence becomes ever more apparent.

Companies specializing in 'adventure holidays' are already exploiting the more accessible of the world's deserts – though by their very nature, organized holidays, with the primary need for guaranteeing the safety of clients can never hope to offer more than a glimpse of the true potential of the desert experience, which is essentially a solitary exploration. Nonetheless, people are captivated by the romance of the desert, and it follows that Jordan should pin its hopes of a larger share of the

world's tourist trade on such places as Wadi Rum, described by
Lawrence of Arabia as 'Vast and God-like', and which was the
one place I felt I had to see.

Wadi Rum is typical of much of Jordan's spectacular
southern deserts, an immensely wide flat-floored sandy canyon
in which sparse occasional rains produce a little vegetation. The
sense of vastness which is indeed the most immediate and
abiding impression, is as much due to the massive flanking cliffs
which dwarf man and everything else to insignificance. Similar
canyons lead off the main wadi at intervals, each splitting into
an infinity of smaller valleys, all with their own amazing rock
formations. The whole complex spreads over many square miles
before merging into the flat sands of the deserts of Arabia. It is
terrain where a traveller could wander for weeks, months even,
without seeing another soul. The sudden longing to change all
my plans, hire a camel and set off into the heart of this majestic
country was very strong. I had to remind myself very firmly that
this journey had a different purpose.

There was really time only to experience the initial impact of
Wadi Rum, just half a day and one night. I was set down at
midday, outside the Government Rest House a little way up the
wadi. My driver, Mahmoud could barely wait to drop me off
before turning the Mercedes' nose in the direction of the flesh-
pots of Aqaba where he proposed to spend the night. He
thought I was mad to prefer a tent in the sand which was the
accommodation offered by the rest house.

A Bedouin village lay just beyond this rest house, its purpose
to exploit the infant tourist trade by ferrying visitors around the
major sights of Wadi Rum in four-wheel drive trucks. I turned
down this opportunity of going further and seeing more,
knowing from experience that I would get a better idea of the
place by just trudging off on my own feet. In any case I was in
need of exercise after all this ferrying around in the Mercedes.

Walking was a struggle through the deeply-churned sand,
the result of the erosion of the valley floor by the fleet of
Bedouin trucks and the excessive flocks of goats bought with
the proceeds of the tourist trade. The Jordanian authorities had
at last realized that the marvellous but fragile habitat was fast

disappearing under the onslaught, and plans were afoot to move the village further down the wadi.

There was no way that the unprotected sand could cope with the passage of even a few motor vehicles or with the numbers of camels that would be needed to replace them. I had been told of grand plans for a circular train, hot air balloon flights, and miles and miles of protected walkways – projects that awaited massive funding. I was glad I was seeing it now before these necessary, but sad changes would be in force.

Across the wadi, trailing a small cloud of dust, a Bedouin woman hurried homewards with her flock. At my feet delicate wild cyclamen were still managing a tenuous hold among the multitude of deep intersecting wheel ruts. No other visitors were to be seen. Once the village and the herdswoman were behind me, I had the whole wadi to myself. The silence and the grandeur gripped me in so powerful a hold that I felt a rising of the spirit that lies at the heart of all worship. 'Alluha ad Akbar', Great indeed is God.

On either side of the immensely wide valley floor, along which I trudged, rose the great rock walls, the canvas where ancient races had scratched their records of the hunt and the outlines of animals on which their lives depended. The same cliffs had become the latest arena for some of the newest and most challenging of rock climbs. For those quick enough off the mark there is the rare opportunity of putting up entirely new routes on these red cliffs. As the pitons are fixed, the pegs driven in, another of the world's inviolate fastnesses will be conquered and the awful silence broached.

I thought of previous centuries when the growth of the early Christian Church had also brought a new and sudden popularity to deserts. At that time they were not considered peaceful retreats, but places that teemed with demons. Not only were there the inner demons every man brought with him, but also the external forces, the 'Hosts of Satan', the 'powers and principalities'. It was to wrestle with both his own sins and the greater forces of evil that the Desert Fathers, such as St Jerome had sought such places. So widespread became this practice of withdrawing to the desert that it led eventually to the great monastic movements of Christianity.

Without the leisure for sitting and musing there was no question of my wrestling with any demons. Instead I felt ravished by the beauty and the splendour of it all, as the flush of a desert sunset burnished the towering cliffs, and the side valleys to the east grew sombre and mysterious with dark, lengthening shadows.

From this wadi T. E. Lawrence had organized his Bedouin for the daring attack on the Turkish stronghold at Aqaba. I had recently been re-reading his *Seven Pillars of Wisdom*, and being in a place so closely associated with him, I felt an even greater nostalgia for the freedom of the desert which he had so profoundly valued, and which I saw as about to change forever.

I walked back down the valley under bright starlight thinking about the Arab world to whose leaders Lawrence, and others like him, had made such golden promises. Perhaps his growing bitterness as, one by one, those promises had been broken were what led to the strange course Lawrence's life subsequently followed, rather than what might or might not have been done to him by the Turks. El Orance! In spite of those broken promises, his memory is still honoured in these parts, for Arabs tend to judge a man by the goodness of his heart, and Lawrence's own loyalty was never in doubt.

From thinking about Lawrence, it was a natural step to consider present-day Jordan, and the future of the descendants of those Arabs whose cause Lawrence had espoused.

I had been told a great deal over the past few days about Jordan's plans for future prosperity, and the pattern of these was now becoming clear. The Peace Treaty itself was a simpler matter, for it had seemed clear from the first that after Egypt had made its peace with Israel, it could only be a matter of time before the rest of the Arab world, and Jordan in particular, would have to follow suit.

The most pressing incentive for Jordan to achieve peace with Israel was the state of her economy. Her international debts were crippling, and a massive influx of fresh international investment was desperately needed. Water was at an even greater crisis point. Jordan's share of the rivers of the region had been syphoned off by Israel until there was not enough even for the basic everyday needs of the people, let alone for urgent irrigation purposes.

Water has always assumed great importance in these parts, but the increasing shortage of it in modern times has imbued it with an almost sacred quality, as was well illustrated the day I was visiting the desert castles with an eminent archaeologist. We had arrived at Lawrence's former desert headquarters, the ancient fort of Azraq, a wonderfully primitive place with solid rock doors a metre thick that swung on their own massive pintles in sockets of granite, just as Hittite and Babylonian gates had done. The fort was so austere and so totally lacking in anything that might be construed as comfort that I felt a new surge of respect for T. E. Lawrence.

Azraq's other claim to fame was in having the only permanent natural standing water in Jordan. It was in fact a true oasis and the broad expanse of it looked wonderful, as a lake of water always does in the desert, with the strange refracting quality of the air around it and the unaccustomed flurry of bird life. I could not quite understand, however, why the staid archaeologist was embracing Mahmoud, and why both were jumping up and down with delight at the sight of it, until they stopped to explain that the lake had been dry for all but a day or two over the last few years, and that neither had ever before seen it full like this. I wondered then whether water alone, without any other considerations, was not enough to dictate the terms of peace in these dry lands.

One of the main obstacles to negotiating any peace had been the anomalous position of Jordan with regard to the Palestinians and their territory. Only after the PLO had been officially recognized as the sole representative of the Palestinian peoples was that obstacle removed. Jordan's role as an umbrella for Palestinian negotiations could then be put aside. After 1988 and the final severing of all legal and administrative links between the two peoples, Palestinians could affirm their rights to their land in their own name.

The one responsibility Jordan retained in Palestine was the custodianship of the Holy Places of Jerusalem which had been under King Hussein's charge since 1948. This he felt was too precious and important to relinquish until it could be handed over intact to a stable and established Palestinian regime. Apart from this, after the official separation both peoples were free to pursue their own negotiations directly with Israel.

The Jordan/Israel Peace Treaty which was signed in October 1994 guaranteed a wiping out of the major part of Jordan's debts to America and the Western world. It also promised Jordan a fair share of the waters of the region, and the return of the small pockets of land occupied by Israel since 1948. Jordan's borders were also properly defined for the first time. The rest of the package – an inflow of investment capital, establishment of regional development projects, the end of Jordan's political and economic isolation, and co-operation with Israel on joint ventures in the Jordan Valley – were, it would seem, rather vaguer promises, that might or might not be honoured. Most Jordanians I met casually, who were not setting out the official line, shared this view.

'We are still waiting to see the difference,' was the response of most people I talked with. Nearly everyone endorsed the idea of peace, but very few trusted it. Israel to most Jordanians was the big 'grab-all' country of the Middle East, and they could not see her parting with anything she wanted for herself. 'Look at Egypt,' they said. 'She made her peace first, and what happened? Within a year Israel had taken over Egypt's entire egg trade. Not one single egg is now produced in Egypt. Israelis get richer at the expense of others.'

I put this point to most of the ministers and the university professors I was meeting. 'How,' I would ask, 'can you hope to compete with Israel who has such a head start technically and industrially, as well as the massive financial backing of America?'

The invariable response was that Jordan's strength was flexibility, and the valuable training of having had to survive almost entirely by her own efforts. Israel was dependent on massive external funding, largely American, which made for an inherent weakness in the Israeli economy.

Jordan's chief asset in any competition, I was told, was her pool of human resources. For the last twelve years, all the money available had been ploughed into education, nearly all of it in the field of applied science. Everything was focused on the needs of industry. All research projects were self-funding, paid for by the industry that benefited from that particular work. Jordanians' skills were beginning to be employed all over the Arab world as well as further afield. The money the exiles earned mostly came back to swell Jordan's economy.

It all sounded so well worked out and optimistic, that in the waves of enthusiasm it was easy to forget the scale of the problems, as well as the knife-edge nature of peace in this part of the world. Sometimes when I voiced my doubts I struck a responsive chord. 'When you consider the odds stacked against Jordan, what prevents you sinking into complete despair?' I would ask. After the slight hesitation in which the unthinkable abyss gaped, the answer would come: 'The King. It is his courage and his persistence that has kept all of us going for over forty years. He will not allow us to give up hope. And his brother, Crown Prince Hassan works just as unsparingly.' Remembering the King's words to me in England, 'What other choice do we have? What sort of world do we want to leave to our children and our grandchildren?' I felt I understood a little of their optimism.

King Hussein was put forward as Jordan's prime asset more often than could be accounted for by anything other than an overwhelming respect that spilled over into love. He had earned this respect, I was assured, it was not just an accident of birth. While there was a great deal more scepticism on the streets than at official levels, the respect for the king was much the same and was possibly the most cohesive factor in the country. Over and over again I was told simply, 'He is the father of his people.'

A typical unofficial airing of such views was one I enjoyed while being invited to drink tea in the forecourt of the small museum in Aqaba. About eight men were present, from the cleaner and gardener to the curator himself, for everywhere I found Jordan wonderfully un-class conscious, with no one shy to speak his mind.

'Peace?' said one, 'Today I am for it, but maybe tomorrow I will change my mind.'

'Salem changes his mind every day, as many of us do, depending on the newspapers and the latest developments,' said another.

'At first I was for peace, and still I think it is right because I trust our King,' said Salem, 'but the longer we wait and nothing happens, the less I believe in it. Where are the benefits we were promised? I do not trust Israel, I do not trust the West. We have been let down too many times.'

The atmosphere, I thought, was one of truce rather than an agreed peace. If the current peace was to have any reality it was clear that there had to be immediate and tangible benefits, and like the Jordanians themselves, I could not see any as yet.

Tourism, I was told by the relevant minister, also features high in Jordan's future projected economy. Up until now most visitors to Jordan have tacked a quick visit onto a Holy Land tour, with Israel as the base and the chief beneficiary. Jordan certainly has enough to offer on its own account, and tourists I met in Aqaba, who had just crossed the new border from Israeli Eilat, all expressed their delight at finding the Jordanian side far pleasanter, cleaner and altogether friendlier.

But Jordan's tourist industry awaits a large investment programme, as well as the funds to protect such easily damaged places as Wadi Rum. So far only the 'rose-red city' of Petra can be claimed as a reasonable money spinner, and even that is not without its problems.

At my request Mahmoud had driven me down to Wadi Rum along part of the Kings Highway where years before I had come by bicycle, almost drunk with the marvels I was seeing. Older now and with less muscle power I wondered where I had found the strength to tackle the profound rocky ravine of Wadi Mujib. The Crusader castles and the thrilling rocky landscape through which the Children of Israel had wandered during their forty years in the wilderness were all more or less as I remembered them, although nowhere near as exciting of course, because I was not travelling under my own steam. Only Petra had changed.

Where previously had stood one solitary newly-built hotel among a few very amateur souvenir and fake antiquities stalls, was now a small modern town totally dedicated to the entertainment of visitors to Petra. The 'rose-red city' itself, hidden away at the end of the long winding high-walled siq is doubtless very little changed. But I had enjoyed the privilege of seeing it much as the Victorian explorers had done. I had the place to myself and had slept in an ancient tomb among the ruins, a guest of the Bedouin who had lived there for generations, and from whose black tents refreshing glasses of mint tea were produced in gestures of age-old hospitality. The quality of such a visit cannot be repeated. There was no point in diminishing the experience by scrambling around it again in company with hundreds of others.

But even Petra, popular though it has undoubtedly become, is in no way the bread winner it should be. All the time that it was out of bounds to Israel, it was a lodestone, a forbidden city that all Israelis, particularly the young, longed to get to. A piece of the red rock of Petra was a prized possession for which the most foolhardy were prepared to risk their lives. Now there was peace, coupled with the new border crossing at Aqaba, the Israelis flooded in.

The trouble was they could get there and back again easily in a day, without spending anything in Jordan other than the entrance fee to the ruins. A new rule, hastily drawn up, which required tourists to exit by a different crossing to the entry point did little to mend matters, for distances were really small enough for a determined visitor to still avoid spending even a single night in Jordan.

When I bicycled there I had found several days too short for Petra, but rushing about in cars and buses undoubtedly gave one a different perspective on exploration. I had visited more sites in the Mercedes, between meetings, than I had done in the entire time I had spent in Jordan previously, and I was grateful for the opportunity. But as I slogged the last few hundred yards through the deep tiring sand I was also profoundly glad to have been able to make this first acquaintance with Wadi Rum alone and under my own steam.

Thinking about the information I had accumulated over the past two weeks I had felt a strange link between Jordan's hopes and aspirations and the nature of this lovely wadi I had just wandered through. In spite of all the strictly utilitarian ideas and the economic emphases that had been expounded to me by experts and politicians, Jordan still struck me as a nation of desert idealists. Surrounded on all sides by richer neighbours, with no natural resources worth talking about, what did they have but this God-like natural wilderness and their courage and will to succeed? I wished them well.

Stumbling into the lights of the rest house I found a very anxious Mahmoud just preparing to organize a search party to look for his foreign charge. Something, possibly a higher authority, had caused him to change his mind about staying the night in Aqaba, and he had returned to the rest house only to find that I was still somewhere out there in the desert, several hours after darkness had fallen. The discovery had clearly shaken him badly. Coming of Bedouin stock, he should have known better, as I told him. I had a compass with me as well as a torch, though I had needed neither in such clearly defined and recognizable terrain, and under such bright desert starlight.

Dear Mahmoud, his relief was such that he went around boasting to everyone who would listen, including the putative search party, all about his English client who was 'truly a free person, and who knew how to walk alone in the desert with a compass and a torch'.

The rest house, a soulless building, got up to look vaguely like the interior of a Bedouin tent, was doomed to failure by the uncompromising barn-like architecture and neon lighting. The atmosphere was not helped by the cold, which had turned positively arctic once the sun was down. The indifferent food, however, was helped by some excellent beer, and once the insistent rhythm of two local musicians had raised the pulse-rate, the evening brightened. Several other people had booked in while I had been coming down the wadi. There was an Israeli trio of two very pretty North African youths accompanied by a lighter-skinned older man with a loud voice, and a party of four elderly

Austrians in fleece jackets, all deeply immersed in their guide-
books.

The Israeli youths rose to dance, gyrating rather half-
heartedly but provoking no response from their companion.
Mahmoud who had been twitching in time with the music rose
instead and flung himself joyfully into the by now frenzied beat.
Several off-duty policemen from the local barracks also joined
in, each vaguely relating to another dancer while really
immersed in his own steps. It was like the dancing I remembered seeing in Egyptian villages, the same self-absorbed attention. These Jordanians were also a delight to watch, surprisingly
graceful and quite without the least self-consciousness, though
Mahmoud seemed to be adding a touch of Western style to his
efforts.

The big surprise was when one of the elderly Austrian
women rose and, with great dignity combined with an
admirable sinuousness of the hips and no small degree of skill,
joined in the sensuous movements of the Arab dance. One of
the policemen partnered her, and after a short but impressive
exhibition she sat down to prolonged applause. Mahmoud
wildly excited at the unexpected turn of events begged me to
come and gyrate too, but to my shame I simply could not. I was
just as inhibited as the older Israeli, who also continued to resist
the enticements of his dark-skinned companions. The situation
was saved by the Austrian woman, who kindly rose again to give
Mahmoud the benefit of a female focus for his wild gyrations.
'It is easy,' she said, shrugging, as I expressed my admiration. 'I
work with Palestinian refugees and they teach me; you have
only to wriggle your hips about a bit.'

On that note the party broke up and we few guests braved
the impressive cold of the bright desert night in a dash to the
tents. I, thank goodness, had already donned my thermals, and
with my excellent lightweight sleeping-bag to add to the
warmth of the half-dozen blankets provided, soon dozed off.

I slept well, the sense of the majesty of the place permeating
my dreams.

CHAPTER NINE

Crossing Over Jordan

From Mount Nebo, high above the Jordan Valley I thought I could just make out the glint of the golden Dome of the Rock in Jerusalem. Pale thin images wavering and fragmenting in the haze were the towers and minarets of the Holy City that I imagined I could fix from memory, for I had stood on this mountain on a brighter clearer day when the roofs of Jerusalem and Bethlehem, thirty miles to the west, were clearly visible.

It was to this view point that Moses climbed in order to feast his eyes on the land of Canaan in the final days of the wanderings of the Children of Israel. Like Abraham before him, Moses was not destined to set foot in the Promised Land, but died here in Moab after gazing across the great sweeping panorama that lay before me. Moses is said to be buried in an unidentified cave somewhere in the honeycomb hillside below, making the mountain the most holy biblical site in Jordan.

A Christian church has commemorated the spot since the fourth century, when Constantine the Great adopted Christianity as Rome's official religion, and his mother, the indefatigable Empress Helena, rushed off to Palestine to identify all the major biblical places, and to begin the process of building basilicas over them.

The Franciscans who are responsible for many of the Holy Land archaeological sites have excavated a succession of Christian buildings on Mount Nebo. The earliest of them, a tiny trefoil church built of large decorated stone blocks was mentioned by the pilgrim Egeria when she visited the site in AD 390, when it was apparently in the charge of Egyptian monks. Beautiful mosaic floors also came to light in the excavations, for the Byzantines were particularly skilled in this art form, and fine examples of their work abound in Western Jordan. The nearby town of Madaba which was particularly rich in both Christian churches and mosaic floors has given its name to a unique map in this medium which is possibly the most famous in the world.

I had stopped at Madaba on the way to Mount Nebo in order to take another look at this marvellous map which was made around the year AD 560 and conceived on a grand scale. Over two million mosaic cubes went into its construction and in its finished state it measured some five metres wide by twenty-five metres long, dimensions that matched the narrow land of biblical Palestine. Its range extended from the Nile Delta to Sidon, with Jerusalem set at the centre, complete with its main Roman street, the Cardo. Principal towns were shown, together with geographical features such as hills and valleys, and also details of flora and fauna – lions apparently still roamed freely in Moab in the sixth century, as they had done twelve hundred years before in the days of Jeremiah.

According to the inscription on the map, the work (11,500 hours of it one authority suggests) was all paid for by the 'Christ-loving people of this town of Madaba'. It is the only ancient map of Palestine in existence, which makes it all the more appalling that great portions of it have been wantonly destroyed.

The Madaba Map was still almost intact until the final decade of the last century when a monk wrote to the Greek Patriarch in Jerusalem to inform him of the existence of the priceless mosaic masterpiece. No one in authority expressed much interest at the time, and it was only after a lapse of several years that an architect was sent to build a church over the map, apparently with the idea of incorporating the work into the pavement of the new building. Clearly right hand had lost touch with left during the delay, because in the interest of his own design the architect saw fit to obliterate large parts of the mosaic. The final irony is that the church itself, an ugly building without any distinction whatsoever, has become famous because of housing the priceless remnants of the Madaba Map.

By good fortune, the section showing Jerusalem is one part that has survived, and as I stood looking at it I marvelled again at the skill of the unknown artist who could create so basically utilitarian a work that nonetheless sparkled with animation fourteen centuries later. It made me eager to be back in Jerusalem walking this very Cardo, which now lies some twenty feet below street level of today's Holy City. The thought of it caused the same sudden change in heartbeat as I now felt looking out over the Jordan Valley from Mount Nebo.

For lovely though the ruins of the successive churches are, the focus of Mount Nebo lies outwards. There are few places on earth where landscape and history combine so dramatically. Nothing in the huge panorama is ordinary; everywhere the eye wanders is charged with significance. The pale and intensely blue expanse of the Dead Sea lies immediately below. At 400 metres below sea-level it is the lowest spot on earth and, to my eyes, looks as weirdly and malignantly lifeless as its name. It fascinates and repels at the same time. That the destroyed cities of Sodom and Gomorrah were built along its shores seems only fitting, and I find it tempting to imagine that the lake suffered its fate in the same cataclysmic event.

The brilliant green of the fertile Jordan Valley begins abruptly at the northern edge of the Dead Sea, while far away to the south the blue merges gradually into the darkening yellow haze of the Negev Desert. Sun-bleached inhospitable cliffs rising abruptly beyond the Dead Sea's margins are riven with occasional green ravines where springs of fresh water support life. Caves adjacent to these oases were once frequented by ascetic religious sects like the Essenes, whose writings carefully stored in pottery jars, lay preserved for hundreds of years before a shepherd boy stumbled upon them and added the Dead Sea Scrolls to the world of biblical scholarship.

Jericho is out of sight, but above, high on the western bank where the cliffs flow without interruption into the folded Judaean Wilderness is the place marked by a monastery where tradition claims Jesus spent his forty days in the desert. Of the River Jordan little is visible, and certainly not the traditional site of the Baptism of Christ, but the place where Salome danced before Herod for the head of John the Baptist is not far away, on this side of the Jordan in the fortress of Machaerus.

The entire perspective is on the grand scale, as the setting for such a drama should be. But thrilling, savage, deeply evocative though it all undoubtedly is, what repeatedly drew my eye back was the glint of sunlight thirty miles away striking fire from Jerusalem.

To reach this, the promised goal, was once more proving no easy passage. I had begun my arrangements for crossing the Israeli border almost as soon as I had arrived in Amman. The British Embassy implied that endless complications still remained the order of the day, and as far as they were aware, the embargo on bicycles had not been lifted. They advised me to check arrangements with the newly established Israeli Embassy.

I rang the person whose name I had been given. 'Put it in a telex,' he said, and rang off abruptly. I did so and heard no more until about ten days later when a young woman telephoned me at the Inter-Continental.

'OK,' she said without preamble, 'you can cross with your bike, but not by the Allenby Bridge. You have to go to Sheikh Husseini instead.'

'Where is that?' I asked.

'I don't know,' she replied. 'I was just told to tell you.'

'Can I have something in writing?' I inquired, remembering the misery of the previous crossing, when in spite of all the high-level negotiations and ensuing promises, the Israelis at the Allenby Bridge had still claimed to know nothing of the arrangements. An official document would take a great weight off my mind.

'You don't need anything,' said the young voice, airily. 'We checked up on you with London, and it's OK.'

'But what if I have trouble at the bridge?' I put in quickly, before she too could slam down the phone.

'Oh yes,' she said. 'Then you must ask for Mr Motti Baraam.' And with that I had to be content for she had rung off.

A name is better than nothing. I just hoped I had heard it right. Tomorrow, presumably, I would find out.

The Sheikh Husseini turned out to be a newly constructed

pontoon bridge inconveniently located way up in the very north of Jordan, almost level with the Sea of Galilee. It meant a doubling back on my tracks of a hundred miles and more. Then, if I succeeded in getting over the River Jordan, I would have to double back again on the other side as far as the Allenby Bridge, before beginning the long haul up to Jerusalem. It seemed an entirely pointless exercise. Had there been any attempt to explain why an inconvenience of two hundred miles was necessary it would have helped. As it was it appeared to be just the usual bureaucratic bloody-mindedness.

None of my Jordanian contacts could understand it either, and the palace representative in the hotel tried her best to get permission for me to use the Allenby Bridge, but with no success. In the end, since my time was so limited, it was decided that both luggage and bicycle could be fitted in the capacious boot of the Mercedes, and Mahmoud could drive me up to the Sheikh Husseini Bridge.

I had planned this visit to Mount Nebo for my last day in Jordan because it is so appropriate a point to take one's leave of the country. But standing here now with Jerusalem in my sights and knowing that I would have to cover at least seven times the distance to reach it, the madness of the situation struck me afresh. O for Elijah's Chariot of Fire – or even a more prosaic hot-air balloon.

These reveries were broken in upon by Mahmoud reminding me that it was time to leave for Jordan's television studios where I had agreed to be interviewed for the early evening news programme. It seemed to me a good opportunity to say 'Thank you' for all the hospitality I had received in the country, as well as to put in a plug for the joys of bicycling, little though two-wheeled travel had featured on this visit to Jordan.

It was raining when we left Amman the following morning and everyone was smiling because rain is so welcome and so infrequent. Since I had not succeeded in losing the receipt Roberts was released from the dark cupboard and loaded, with some difficulty, into the Mercedes. Bits of handlebar and wheels stubbornly refused to go in, and string was necessary to tie down the boot lid, all of which rather spoilt the dignity of

Mahmoud's pride and joy. The friendly staff of the Inter-Continental watched the proceedings from the shelter of the lobby and I was glad of the rain which made farewells mercifully brief.

The wide cement city was soon far behind us and we swept back over the hills of Gideon, with a great deal more ease than I had managed on Roberts. Like a dream, great misty hills loomed up across the rift of the Jordan with an opening in the clouds above them sending down beams of watery sunlight to gild the visions of a promised land.

Four hours after leaving Amman Mahmoud dropped me at a gate manned by Jordanian soldiers. While I straightened the wheel and strapped on the panniers, he boasted, as he always did, about his client. This time I was not only a 'truly free woman' who went all over the world with her bicycle. I had also been on television. They had seen it? Was it not good? His eulogies possibly eased the first part of the long approach to the bridge, but they did not reach far enough. At the next gate a small man came running out, arms flailing.

It was difficult to find a break in his speech, which was all about bicycles not being allowed. When he did finally pause for breath I said politely that this bicycle was allowed. But that only set him off on another long speech about his knowing exactly what the Israelis would and would not permit. Jordan was working closely with Israel, and he was in charge of this side of the crossing.

Had I managed to procure the written Israeli authorization I had wanted, I could have put it in his hand and waited quietly until he had taken in its import. The problem was he thought he had to persuade me that it was not Jordan's fault, but Israel's that bicycles were 'machina non grata'. I, of course, already knew this and was wondering how to make him change tack, or to pause long enough for me to explain. Eventually I found the place in my notebook where the name 'Motti Baraam' was carefully written. When I uttered this name aloud the little man stopped speaking and looked at me suspiciously. I repeated firmly: 'Mr Motti Baraam will tell you I am allowed to cross.'

'Motti is my friend,' he said. 'Same as I am here, he is over there.'

'Well, you ask him,' I said, hoping desperately that this time someone really had got their act together; at least the name was right!

Telling me firmly to wait and not move he went off to telephone my unlikely story to the other side. The wait was not long. Saving face by saying that had it been anyone else on a bicycle, they would immediately have been sent back where they came from, he beckoned me forward for processing. This too was not without problems. I was to get on a special little bus which would take me the twenty feet across the narrow pontoon bridge. For some inexplicable reason this minute span could not be walked or ridden. The over-laden Roberts was heaved aboard by two strong guards and I was taken to have my passport stamped. At this point it was revealed that I had to pay an exit tax, the first time I had ever had to do so when leaving a country by road. Not expecting it I had got rid of all my spare dinars in tips at the hotel. Turning out my pockets I held out the small handful of coins which remained. 'Motti's friend' said this would do for the bus, but much more was needed for the tax, and traveller's cheques would not do, it must be currency. Another search revealed my last few emergency dollars, and only after these had been converted into dinars and then paid over was my passport stamped and myself directed to join Roberts in solitary splendour on the bus.

A modern version of Charon the Ferryman climbed in behind the steering wheel and held out his hand for the fare. No sooner had I tipped into it the remaining coins, as instructed, than he began to call loudly on heaven to witness the unspeakable miserliness of the amount I was proffering. 'Motti's friend' sternly gestured him forward, and almost before I had time to take in the fact that we were moving, we were over the Jordan (which is neither deep nor wide as the song would have us believe) and the door had swung open ready for me to descend.

The floor of the bus was high off the ground and there was no possibility of my lifting Roberts down without help. A burly girl in the grey uniform of the Israeli security service had sprung forward the moment the bus stopped and stood below the entrance, armed and unsmiling. 'Could you give me a hand down with this please?' I said with my best attempt at charm, 'I can't manage it on my own.' To my astonishment she turned on me such a look of malevolence that she appeared actually to snarl before turning away and spitting.

While I was recovering from the shock of this, the bus driver, who had so recently castigated my unwitting meanness, walked round, and not only lifted down the bicycle but also insisted on shaking my hand. I took it that he was showing me some sort of solidarity, but there are times when a traveller cannot hope to make sense of events. The last time I crossed the River Jordan there had been a man who, piece by piece, was hurling a huge pile of shiny new aluminium pots and pans into the water in another equally inexplicable symbolic gesture.

Safely set down on 'Camp Ground', 'Canaan's Shore' or, in modern political terms, Israeli territory, other grey-uniformed girls closed in around us and instructed me to wheel Roberts into an office; it seemed that this time I was expected. The grey-clad branch of the Israeli security service which is largely composed of young women, is well-known and seldom loved by people who visit Israel frequently. It is not the security measures which are objected to. A country so subject to terrorist attacks needs tight security, and it is a relief to see a rigorous baggage inspection enforced. But what is irritating and also pointless is the third degree questioning to which anyone, from eminent professors, aid workers and church personnel to visiting travellers like myself are subjected by these often rude young women, who seldom pause long enough to hear the answers. 'Give us the names of the people you have been meeting while in Israel,' or 'Who have you talked to while you were here?' are the type of demands to which it is only natural to object.

At some point in the cross-examination the question will be put: 'You understand why we are asking these questions?' Those who respond, quite rightly, with something to the effect of 'Anything to do with security I will gladly tell you, but you have no right to subject me to a cross-examination about my private affairs,' can find themselves in real trouble. Depending on the pressure of work, the ego of the questioner, or an arbitrary quota system, the one-sided harassment will either stop and the person be free to proceed to the departure lounge, or he will be marched off to 'the little room' to be more thoroughly humiliated by a detailed body search. Since the real Israeli security is a highly sophisticated affair, it is difficult to imagine that there is any practical purpose in these ad hoc 'security procedures'.

I had steeled myself for this encounter so as to remain calm in the face of provocation, but to my surprise I was treated with an exaggerated politeness that was taken to the point of embarrassment. There were apologies for the necessity of inspecting my panniers, apologies for having to feed Roberts upside down through the X-ray machine, none of which I considered other than perfectly reasonable and routine. One girl seemed on the point of tears because she could not remember the order in which she had taken the things out of my bags. When I said I didn't in the least mind and was happy to repack it myself, she replied despondently that she should remember as it was her job. I began to wonder if Israel had indeed had a massive change of heart because of the recent peace moves, or whether the criticism from Jewish newspapers about Israel's public relations image had at last been noted. But I think it was really because I had told the Israeli Cultural Attaché in London about my previous unfortunate experiences in crossing the Allenby Bridge, and they did not want me to write such an anti-tourist account this time.

Passport control showed a flash of the old Israeli style which was almost refreshing after the waves of stifling bonhomie. Many countries will not accept a passport which shows that the holder has visited Israel, and this has not been changed by the recent peace initiatives. If a traveller has any intention of moving freely around the world it is necessary to ask for the Israeli entry stamp to be put on a separate piece of paper. I had never before been refused this request, but to my surprise on this occasion I was told it could only be done if I had good reason, and if 'the boss' said it was OK. I wondered if this 'boss' might be the powerful and so far invisible Mr Motti Baraam.

I explained about being a writer and a traveller and needing to pass through all manner of countries, and from the back recesses came the disembodied question: 'Can she prove it?' As I was bringing a copy of one of my books for a Jerusalem friend I said I thought I could and fished it out of a pannier. Several Israeli bystanders gathered around to have a look and to comment over the photograph of Eastern Turkey on the cover; one said he thought he had seen this book for sale in a shop, which was encouraging, for it is always good to know that one's books are earning money abroad. But I was more interested in showing the official that the name on the cover matched the name in my passport and that the picture of me on the flyleaf also tallied. She took them into the back office from where I heard the voice say sourly: 'A card with writer on it was all I was asking for.'

Now that the fraught business of the crossing was behind me and I was free to take in lesser matters I was aware of the steady drizzle and the cold wind blowing around the bleak border buildings. One of these temporary sheds housed a bank where at a little outside window offering no shelter from the elements I changed a traveller's cheque, nearly getting blown away in the process. But it was worth it for the comfort that having the right currency gives: credit cards and cheques are no substitute for cash. With shekels in my pocket I could get a meal and shelter, or even a bus to Jerusalem. For now I was so close I could not bear the thought of further delay.

The town of Beit Shean was fairly close and I thought I would cycle there and see if there was a bus going in vaguely the right direction. If I could get a lift at least as far as Jericho I could be in Jerusalem by nightfall.

The long gentle climb out from this northern end of the Jordan Valley warmed me up by the time I reached Beit Shean. Only the strategic position of this early Bronze Age town on its watchful ridge and a few heaps of ancient stone give any hint of its long, involved history or of the many layers of successive occupation. Once a wall of the town bore the dead stripped body of King Saul, nailed there by the victorious Philistines. Now that Beit Shean has become the Jewish centre of the Jordan Valley, brash plastic and concrete is replacing all but the finest of the old Arab houses. And because this is truly Israel and not occupied territory there are no Arabs at all to be seen. The native Israelis appeared friendly and relaxed.

By good fortune a bus going all the way to Jerusalem was expected shortly, and when it came it was half empty so there was no difficulty in persuading the driver to take Roberts in the capacious luggage space beneath the seating. The Israeli bus service is excellent and cheap, and as another passenger observed as I climbed wetly aboard and dripped my way down the aisle, at least it wasn't raining inside.

We set off southwards back down the Jordan Valley. It was an infinitely tamer and less lovely prospect, though probably a good deal richer than the side I had just left. Within a few kilometres the bus had entered the occupied West Bank, though there was nothing I could see to mark a border. The main differences were the wealth of high fences and military posts. All along the rich valley floor, the land seemed to be mainly parcelled out into kibbutzim and settlements, and Israelis seemed to be entirely in possession of it. It was winter and nothing much was going on in the fields, so I could not see whether Arab labour was still employed or whether it had been replaced by the new Romanian immigrant workers. The only people getting on and off the bus were Israeli soldiers.

I have cycled the entire valley in the past and thought it lovely, but at the pace of a bus details get blurred and it was not exciting, especially not on a wet, cold day in late January. Worn out by the recent busy schedule and by all the late night reading I fell asleep, and did not surface until the bus was climbing up towards sea level.

Nearing the eastern outskirts of Jerusalem I had one of those unsettling moments of travel when well-remembered places appear suddenly changed out of all recognition, so that you wonder for a moment if you have gone mad, or if the world is playing some monstrous trick. Whole areas of the countryside had disappeared, been swallowed up, and in their place were substantial high uniform white buildings. As the bus circled round towards the west, Jerusalem appeared to be ringed by a great sea of these new settlements; the place looked like a fortress.

Only just before we rolled into the bus station in West Jerusalem did familiar sights restore my faith in Holy Land geography. I pulled Roberts out from his latest cubby-hole and concentrated on fixing the luggage securely, in case in my excitement I left a strap loose to catch in the wheel and unseat me.

Jerusalem, the walled and gated city of the Bible is known in these parts as the 'Old City' to distinguish it from the far larger urban area of modern Jerusalem that spreads outwards from its walls. Just seeing the words 'Old City' written on road signs with lesser place names above and below it, sends a shiver down my spine. It is as though this casual acknowledgement that the city exists, that it lies in a particular direction, changes its status. Jerusalem, an idea in the heart of the individual, becomes a tangible place, a Jerusalem open to all mankind. The reality of it cannot but challenge preconceived notions, or even the memories carried away from other visits. No wonder the impulse is to linger, to savour the moment of anticipation, of having the prize so close without entering the lists of inevitable conflict.

From the west, the way to the Old City lies downhill, a fact that often confuses and disappoints first time visitors to the Holy Land who, like me, have been reared on the 'Going up to Jerusalem' psalms. Moreover West Jerusalem, even if it is all but in name the capital of modern Israel, is still small-town and parochial. Its narrow dusty streets and comfortably shabby shops do not appear to offer a suitable avenue of approach to so venerable and holy a place.

But in fact, since medieval times when a far safer and faster sea passage replaced the long overland route, this was the way the majority of Christian pilgrims arrived at the walls of Jerusalem. Landing at the port of Jaffa, a four day journey would bring them over the intervening hills. And when the final ridge was topped, they would see below them on its lower hill, the longed for vision of felicity. At that time the surroundings were more appropriately rural, the view unimpeded, and it must have been a tremendously impressive sight.

I too had approached Jerusalem by this route. Over the years I had become familiar with West Jerusalem and with the long freewheeling descent down the Jaffa Road. I knew many of the shops there. I even remembered some of the worst distortions in the road surface. Because all these things were markers on the way to Jerusalem they were precious, and I could have shed a tear or two at seeing them again, except that I needed dry eyes for the traffic which is probably no more, but certainly no less pushy than the traffic of any city.

CHAPTER TEN

Pilgrims Gate

The widest and possibly the loveliest view of Jerusalem is from across the Kidron Valley where, from an ancient cemetery half way up the Mount of Olives, the Church of Dominus Flevit marks the spot where Jesus wept for the city. But for travellers approaching Jerusalem along this traditional pilgrim route from the west, the first sight of the Holy City is extremely abrupt. The narrow Jaffa Road, hemmed in on either side by indifferent modern buildings, comes to a halt at a busy intersection; and it is not until this point, separated only by two lines of speeding traffic that Jerusalem reveals herself. Suddenly there is open space and a wide expanse of sky; and there, intact and substantial, are the tall, castellated walls and towers.

Even without the associations the sight alone is sufficient to rivet one to the spot. That Jerusalem is so stunningly beautiful hits me afresh each time I come this way. Three thousand years of the rapturous celebration of that beauty, from King David's psalmists onwards, should mean, rationally speaking, that it cannot possibly live up to expectations; and yet somehow it does. I was as captivated as ever, and cold and wet though the day remained, it was no hardship to walk the last two hundred yards under the shadow of the walls, prolonging the moment of arrival.

There is a commonly held belief that when David Ben-Gurion was Israel's leader he wanted the walls of Jerusalem demolished. By letting the Old City merge into the wider suburbs, he reasoned that it would become just an area in the capital of modern Israel, and that interference with Jerusalem's status would cease. At that time the intention of the United Nations to have the Holy City under some sort of international control was a real possibility.

I wonder what difference it would have made if friends of Ben-Gurion had been unable to persuade him to defer the destruction. Jerusalem's walls have been razed on so many other occasions, and the city has shrunk and grown and changed its shape as conditions have demanded. The present walls are young in terms of the three thousand years of the city's history. Suleiman the Magnificent had them built between AD 1536 and 1540, and is credited with ordering the execution of his architect for failing to include Mount Zion within their compass.

The original City of David, a small enclosure on the eastern hill lies entirely outside these latest walls. It is the 'threshing floor' on a little hill to the north of this original settlement that King David 'bought from Ornan the Jebusite, to build an altar to the Lord' that became the foundation stone of Jerusalem. David's son, Solomon, seeking a site to build a temple to house the Ark of the Covenant chose that same threshing floor and extended Jerusalem to include it. Covered by the layers of the centuries, that altar lies within the present confines of the south-eastern corner of the city under Herod the Great's vast temple platform.

Jerusalem continued to expand until its capture by Nebuchadnezzar in 587 BC which resulted in the Babylonian exile and the second wave of the Jewish Diaspora, the first having begun under the Assyrian conquests of the eighth century BC.

Fifty years later, when Persian power replaced Babylonian, and the Jews were allowed to return, only a minority chose to do so. This remnant rebuilt the temple on a smaller scale, and both temple and city remained within the narrow confines of Solomon's city for the next few hundred years.

Alexander the Great's brief appearance in 334 BC brought profound changes in its wake, not least to Jerusalem. Under their new rulers, the Seleucids, Jews were subjected to increasing pressure to conform to Greek culture, and the tyranny and slaughter employed to this end eventually resulted in the famous revolt under Judas Maccabeus.

With their independence regained Jerusalem took on new

life. In spite of the deep divisions and rivalries within the Jewish ruling classes the city grew, and the walls spread northwards and westwards until they encompassed an area four times as big as Solomon's city.

This growth was not halted when Rome took over the reins in 63 BC. Under puppet rulers like Herod the Great, Jerusalem continued to flourish within strong walls until by the time Jesus was born it had just about reached its greatest extent. This city, Jerusalem at its most magnificent, was the city that Jesus wept over. Together with the nation itself, it was to last only for another decade or two.

Following the First Jewish Revolt in AD 66 Caesar ordered the destruction of the most troublesome of all his conquered nations. After the most dreadful of sieges, graphically described by the historian Josephus, Jerusalem fell, its walls were razed, all save for the three great towers of Herod's citadel which were to serve as a memorial to Roman conquest. Judaea was renamed Palestine, and for a while the whole region became a desert.

The Roman city of Aelia Capitolina which arose on the ashes of Jerusalem was barely half the size of the one destroyed. In outline Aelia is the Jerusalem that we have today, with its main arteries still in place, as the Madaba Map shows. It was to grow and to flourish once again under the Byzantines, when Western pilgrims flooded in to worship at the Holy Places identified by the Empress Helena. At that time the City of David and Mount Zion were within the walls.

With the emergence of Islam in the sixth century and the waves of various Muslim conquerors, the Crusaders and the chaos that followed on their heels, the walls of Jerusalem were destroyed and patched together many times before the Ottoman Empire established itself and Suleiman the Magnificent erected the present six-gated ramparts.

Had Ben-Gurion realized his plan to remove these lovely walls, it would have been a tragic act of vandalism, one more in a long line of similar acts. But it could not surely have blotted out the essential spirit of the place. Where Rome's efforts to obliterate the very memory of a people failed how could modern gelignite and bulldozers succeed any more effectively?

The city's history is that of God active in his creation and in so holy and unique a place, the idea of 'the very stones crying out' does not seem so very far fetched.

My short walk brought me to Jaffa Gate, also known as the Gate of the Pilgrims. This was the way by which General Allenby entered the city in 1917 after the Turkish withdrawal. In the long list of nations which have held sway over Jerusalem in the three thousand years since King David won it from the Jebusites, the thirty-one years of the British Mandate is a mere drop in the ocean. But I am glad that General Allenby saw fit to dismount from his horse on that occasion and enter the city on foot, in the same gesture of respect that the Caliph Omar had shown in AD 637 when he came to receive the submission of 'El Quds', 'The Holy', as Jerusalem is still known to the Arabs. Many other conquerors have been less sensitive to the nature of the place.

Having passed through the double turn of this portal the view that presents itself can have changed but little over the centuries, dominated as it is by the vast bulk of Herod's citadel to the right. Herod's three soaring towers remain much as they were in their original state, as do the beautifully worked massive Herodian stones of the walls' lower courses. Rome left those intact to show, it is said, how great a city it had subdued.

Herod's palace which stretched southwards from the citadel was entirely wrecked in the Jewish uprisings of the first century AD, and the huge area on which it stood is now the Armenian Quarter where I would be staying.

Jerusalem is divided into four main quarters: Jewish, Muslim, Christian, and Armenian. Only the Armenian Quarter is in any way enclosed and that is because much of it lies within the Armenian Convent walls. The convent is a city within a city, having a cathedral, churches, housing, schools and seminaries, as well as the Patriarch's residence, the monks' quarters and many extraordinary religious relics, including one of the stones that according to St Luke's Gospel 'would have cried out'.

Originally the convent's function was entirely religious; it housed the monks and provided shelter for the floods of

Armenian pilgrims who came to Jerusalem for the festivals. After the appalling genocide of the Armenians in Turkey during the first two decades of this century, however, a few of the pitiful survivors were given permanent shelter in the convent, and they and their descendants have remained there ever since.

On an earlier visit to Jerusalem I had the good fortune to make the acquaintance of one of these exiled Armenians, Kevork Hintlian (George to his English-speaking friends) – a scholar with a penchant for helping writers, particularly those who share a passion for his adopted city. George has been largely responsible for my growing understanding of the fabric of Jerusalem. Known and respected throughout the diverse religious and secular institutions of this uniquely complex city, he was able to introduce me to most of the relevant authorities, and many doors were opened that I might not even have known existed. To be presented by George was a guarantee of integrity; it meant that people were more prepared to speak their minds openly, confident that they would not be compromised by injudicious reporting.

On my visits to Jerusalem I usually stayed in an apartment in the Armenian Quarter, though not within the walls, since the custom of locking the gates at 10 p.m., which is still rigorously followed, can prove a serious inconvenience. Many old Armenian houses cling to the outside of the convent walls, however, and the income from renting out a room or two in them is increasingly welcomed in these hard times.

My days in Jerusalem usually followed a fairly set pattern. George would call for me after I had been to early mass at Holy Sepulchre and we would go to a café near the Jaffa Gate for breakfast and our first talk of the day, during which George would tell me whom he had arranged for me to meet. We would then go our separate ways and maybe meet again for lunch and further talks. We shared an interest in history, and our friendship has grown to the point where we could continue conversations we left off a year or more before without apparent interruption.

Much as I valued his help and enjoyed his company, however, I had not expected George to be my mentor on this occasion. Jerusalem, its institutions and ecclesiastical vagaries I felt I already knew well enough, thanks to him. I also thought I understood many of the problems of the Palestinians, both Muslims and Christians. What I knew I lacked was a parallel sympathy with the Israeli position.

I had therefore wanted to spend this visit under the wing of the Israelis, in order to try and see the country and its problems from their specific viewpoint. I hoped they would be able to infuse me with their ideas and aspirations as Jordan had done. Only from an inside position did I think I stood any chance of understanding what to the outsider seemed like naked oppression.

While expressing a vague interest in my ideas, however, the sum total of what the Israeli Embassy in London was prepared to do was to supply me with a 'contact' in Jerusalem who would fix up some introductions for me. I had phoned this contact from Amman to tell her the date of my arrival and to find out what she had arranged. Four rabbis, she said, were anxious to talk to me. Four seemed somewhat weighty, but I passed over that and asked who else she had in mind, pointing out the range of people I was meeting in Jordan and the need to strike a similar balance in Israel. Her response of 'What you need other people for? I thought you were writing a religious book!' convinced me that my time in Israel could be used more profitably. So once again it was George to whom I was turning in my attempts to find out the realities of the current situation.

No surprise was expressed at my sudden appearance at the house he shares with his unmarried sister, only a warm welcome. 'We saw you on television last night,' said George, 'so we knew you were on the way.' Apparently Jordanian television is widely watched in the Middle East. Over the next week lots of people would recognize me as having been on the news, which was often to prove useful in breaking the ice.

George is an unusual combination of scholar and practical fixer. Finding friends a place to rent is child's play compared with the delicate negotiations that are called for in a city where the historical rights of church property and privilege are so jealously

guarded. I was surprised therefore to hear him say that apartments were difficult at present – would I mind if I had to spend
a night or two on his sofa?

Even an invitation to enter George's house is unusual, for he
is a fierce defender of his privacy. I felt privileged to be asked,
but nothing could be less suitable than to be his guest, though
not for considerations of propriety. It is actually a very
charming apartment, typical of the quarter and quite large
enough for a family. But George is like many scholars and
cannot bear to throw away the printed word in any form. The
whole place groans under the weight of paper. It is almost
impossible to move other than sideways, for boxes and crates of
books and newspapers which also stand in piles on almost every
surface. I already felt guilty that Roberts was squashed into the
small hallway dripping steadily onto the nearer piles of
newsprint.

Usually I don't mind where I bed down on my travels, but
suitable lodgings are important in Jerusalem. Coping with the
pressures and tensions of what was never an easy city, meeting
people, listening to complex ideas in a variety of languages,
adjusting to the diverse currents of opinion while remaining
open to what the place itself has to offer can be exhausting
work. A quiet retreat for study and reflection is imperative. I
had never known luxury in Jerusalem but I had usually been
able to find the necessary peace to work, and had been able to
rest my head in modest comfort.

'An invasion of Christian Zionists with more money than
sense' was apparently the cause of a present serious shortage in
rented accommodation. America, who has spawned more weird
quasi-religious sects than any country since ancient Babylon,
was also responsible for this one it seemed. Floods of young
brain-washed idealists were descending on Jerusalem in preparation for the imminent 'Second Coming'. They had no time to
lose, because before the apocalyptic event they had to persuade
the Jews to see the error of their ways and to accept Jesus as the
Messiah.

The Jews as the Chosen People of God had a special place
reserved for them in the heavenly hierarchy. It was theirs once

they could be persuaded to turn from their errors. By helping the Jews, Christian Zionists would earn their own place in heaven, at only a slightly lower level than God's Elect.

It all sounded too banal to be believable even for America's Midwest, and as for taking up all the available accommodation in Jerusalem in a slack season, I found it hard to credit. Only later when I began to realize the numbers involved (over ten thousand at a rough estimate), the amounts of money behind it, and how it was so cleverly organized to attract the gullible, I found it deeply sinister.

Adherents were like zombies, clones of the first one I met who approached George and me a few mornings later when we were having breakfast in an Arab café in El Khattab Square.

She was dressed like one of Jerusalem's new Jewish settlers – who are also nearly all American. The emphasis was on modesty, with skirts almost down to the ground worn over long trousers, and hair in a snood. But there were differences. Most noticeable was that the Christian Zionist was painfully thin, her skin was unhealthily blotchy and she did not have five or six children under seven clinging to her skirts which is *de rigueur* for a Jewish settler.

After George had interpreted for her over the cost of some bottled drink she wanted, she said in her Midwest drawl to the café owner, 'And here is a tip for Shabbat,' which was a rather gauche gesture to an Arab. George questioned her kindly to cover the general embarrassment, and she was only too happy to hold forth. I think she imagined she was making converts.

She was seventeen, had not been to 'regular college', but had gone straight from school to Pentecostal Bible School and then been sent out here. She was up at three every morning to read her Bible, she said, and had just been 'weeping for my sin through Isaiah. It just made me realize I was not a Christian.' Her conversation was utterly bizarre and peppered with scraps of Holy Writ delivered in polite conversational tones. 'I am here to help bring this stiff-necked Jewish Chosen Race to accept their True Messiah, Jesus, and to share in the great day of the Second Coming.' 'They shall see Him whom they pierced.' 'Though Israel has played the Harlot, all will be forgiven if she only repents.' And lots more in a similar vein.

She revealed that she knew nothing at all of the last fifty years of struggle, in fact she seemed to know precious little about anything. Her ideas on the current situation were 'Israel is truly God's people and the Arabs are always wanting more land.' What brains she might once have possessed were addled by lack of sleep, an inadequate diet and the vapid drivel with which she'd been stuffed. She teetered on the brink between hallucination and exaltation.

George asked her if she knew that many Arabs were Christians, and that all these ordinary looking people in the café were in fact Arab Christians, and that the café itself was in the Christian Quarter of Jerusalem. 'Well, see . . .' she said, looking a little less sure of herself, 'no one told me about that, I am just here to help the Jews find Jesus.'

This being my first encounter with a Christian Zionist, I felt I had to try and point out certain basic facts about the country, to all of which she listened with rapt attention. Eventually I realized she was prepared to believe anything I or anyone else told her. For a brief spell she had escaped the safety net of her fellow believers and was as malleable as the proverbial clay. I advised her to go and look around and find out a few facts for herself, but whether the poor demented child was even capable of employing her own senses seemed doubtful. The thought of ten thousand such innocents stirring the already muddied water of present-day Israel was terrifying.

In the meantime, however, the problem of where I should stay had been resolved. George had come up with one of his inspired ideas, and after some judicious telephoning it was arranged for me to have a spare room in an Armenian flat rented out to the Swedish Christian Study Centre. In return I would give a public lecture in the Centre about my travels in Eastern Turkey, and another in the Armenian Seminary, for the Armenians. By happy coincidence the book of this recent journey had arrived in Jerusalem just before I had, and it was this which had given George the idea of a lecture. He had already purchased a copy, making the one I had brought him rather superfluous, I thought. 'Not at all,' said George, with his eye as ever to the niceties of diplomacy, 'We will need many of these for gifts to the right people. I will buy all that they have at Steimasky's tomorrow, and they can order more copies in time for the lectures.

'And now,' he continued, 'you can begin your work straight away. Tonight Albert is giving a dinner for the *Independent*'s journalist, Sarah Helm, whom the Israelis have asked to be recalled because they do not like her articles. You must come too and hear what she thinks about the current situation.'

Albert Aghazarian, another Armenian, is a neighbour of George's and a friend since boyhood. An historian by training, he looks rather like an over-staged Shylock who is sharpening his wit rather than his knife for the next verbal riposte. Director of Public Relations at Birzeit University, I know him best as a guide to the less frequented corners of Jerusalem which he can imbue with life so that even the shadows assume guises of the past.

Together with his charming wife, Miriam, and their three children, Albert lives in a pretty but inconvenient house in the Convent where every room opens out of a central outdoor courtyard. This Roman arrangement is fine in the hot Jerusalem summers, but at well over two thousand feet above sea-level, winter in Jerusalem can be as cold as anywhere in Britain. Few homes in the Old City have any but the most rudimentary heating, and Albert's home was further cooled by blasts of freezing air from the courtyard every time a door was opened. Fortunately he is a generous host and the whisky flowed in sufficient quantity to offset the deadly chill.

Still under the heady spell of arrival I was not in the mood for politics, especially not Sarah Helm's. Later when I read some of her articles about the most recent Israeli land seizures and various repressive measures, I thought her a good and courageous reporter. Having been recalled at the Israeli Government's request, together with a French journalist whose views were similarly disapproved of, her paper was transferring her to Brussels. Naturally enough she appeared angry, both about her own situation and about the wider issues involved. The wine and the good food had little chance of mellowing the atmosphere, and there was not the easy sense of companionship I had been looking forward to on my first evening in Jerusalem.

Now I can see that the fault lay largely with me. It was I who was out of step with the company. I did not want to believe in the scenario that Sarah Helm was offering. I needed time to face the growing suspicion that what had brought me out here was at best, a failure, at worst a cynical charade. I was not yet ready to accept that there was no peace.

CHAPTER ELEVEN

A Beleaguered City

I was up and about very early on my first morning in Jerusalem. Either the gloomy talk of the previous evening or the unaccustomed weight of a huge pile of blankets had caused me to awake with a feeling of doom and oppression. Stepping out onto the icy terrazzo floor at least had the effect of driving all thoughts from my mind except the need to get dressed fast.

There is no grand accommodation within the Old City, and the apartment lent me by the Swedish Study Centre with its three bedrooms, simple shower room and small kitchen was perfectly adequate. There was a desk, a small library, and light to work by, but as the only heating in the entire flat was an old-fashioned inefficient two-bar electric fire, it was deathly cold. My hosts had kindly urged me to leave the fire on all night in order to combat the chill that seeped from the ancient stone walls, but I mistrusted the two-prong plug and not wishing to be the cause of the place burning down I made do with raiding the other beds for blankets to augment my sleeping-bag and thermals. Even so it had been an age before my feet thawed and I made a mental note to buy a hot-water bottle.

The immensely thick walls of my new quarters, together with the delicately arched high ceilings, were built to keep out the searing heat of summer and gave away little information about the world outside. Small, deeply-recessed windows looked out only onto narrow courtyards or blank-walled alleyways. It was therefore a lovely surprise on leaving the house the following morning to find yesterday's rain gone and bright winter sunlight bathing the creamy white walls of Jerusalem. The combination of light and colour is so particular, so unique to Jerusalem that it felt like a second homecoming.

It was not yet six o'clock and I shared the streets only with the shy, ubiquitous cats of the city, some of whom were draped along the tops of sheltered walls taking advantage of these first rays of sunshine. Others were still working over the scattered contents of torn plastic sacks set out for the morning garbage collection. Clearly more robust containers would make the job of disposing of the city's waste a good deal easier and more hygienic, but as this was work performed by imported foreign labour, no one had given it much thought, which was a blessing for the cats of course.

Most cities have their secret army of semi-feral cats which keeps the rats at bay, and while Jerusalem cats are neither as large nor as bold as the imperious tabbies of Venice, neither are they quite as timid or underfed as those of Istanbul. Jerusalem cats come in a wider variety of sizes, colours and patterns than is usual too, as though many have taken to the streets but recently, and have not yet established a common identity. Some indeed are not strays at all but simply share the pickings of those that are. I came to know one such double-lifer who, having dined well in the street, could be observed weaving a tortuous route along walls, roofs and drainpipes to balance precariously on the narrow ledge of a small high-set window at which he scratched for admittance. His owner, an elderly Armenian, seemed always to be waiting for his cat's signal. But the truly nomadic cats find Jerusalem a tough unfriendly place, which is why so many of them frequent the Armenian Quarter where they are less likely to be kicked and persecuted.

The cats got little more than a cursory glance from me on this first morning, however, for I needed the time to explore once again the fabric of the city. In three hours George would be calling for me to begin planning the strategy of the visit, deciding who I should meet and how best to go about my fact finding. Once started on the rounds of meetings, visits and reading, my time would be pressured, and I could only hope for the odd hour snatched here and there. It was most fortuitous therefore that I had woken so early and on such a perfect morning.

From my new quarters, tucked up behind the Armenian

Convent's eastern wall, the city sloped steeply downwards to the Dung Gate in the south-eastern corner of the city. By descending a level I could enjoy a fine, unobstructed view. The newly-built Jewish Quarter, bathed in sunshine lay directly below me descending through stepped and terraced streets to the Wailing Wall, the massive wall built by Herod the Great to buttress the western end of his vast temple pavement.

Above the wall, on the terrace itself, was the golden Dome of the Rock, exactly as I remembered it. I thought of the exposed rock of Mount Moriah beneath the dome, where Abraham was believed to have prepared to make the ultimate sacrifice. It seemed to offer the one spot in Jerusalem that was special to all three great faiths who have 'Abraham as their Father'. If only it could become so! It also occurred to me at that moment that perhaps it could have been this very rock that Christ had in mind when he renamed his disciple Simon, Peter – Petrus, 'the rock on which I shall build my church'.

In order to create a flat area large enough for his grand temple, Herod had the site around the summit of Mount Moriah levelled, shoring up the ground with a series of enormously strong arches, walls and buttresses. Two terraces were thus created; one with a small section of the exposed mountain as its core was a little higher than the other. Over this rock, its holy of holies, Herod's temple arose, and to judge from contemporary accounts it was as magnificent as the enormous expenditure merited. It was also strictly reserved for the use of Jews. A high wall divided the sacred areas from the pavement, and on each of the thirteen gates was the inscription: 'Any gentile entering this barrier will have only himself to blame for his ensuing death'. It was of this temple that Jesus said 'There shall not be left there one stone upon a stone.'

And indeed Herod's magnificent structure stood for less than a hundred years. After the Roman destruction of the city in AD 70, it was replaced by a temple to Jupiter, to which the Romans, slightly more tolerant than Herod, allowed Jews access for a single day in the year in order that they might 'anoint a pierced rock'.

To the Byzantines the great pavement with its Jewish and

pagan associations was a place accursed and they wanted nothing to do with it. For three hundred years it was used as the rubbish dump of the city until the Caliph Omar walked into Jerusalem in AD 638. Horrified by the state of so sacred a site – doubly sacred because it was from this place that Muhammad had leapt to heaven on his charger – Omar ordered the pavement cleared before building a simple shrine over the sacred rock of Mount Moriah. The Temple Mount had become el Haram esh-Sharif, the Noble Sanctuary, an exclusively Muslim place of worship.

The marvellous golden-domed octagonal building that graces the pavement today was erected fifty years after Omar's visit by Caliph Abd-al-Malik, and has withstood the ravages of time and earthquake wonderfully well. The El-Aqsa Mosque which was built on the lower platform seventy years later has not been so fortunate. This is because the Dome of the Rock stands squarely on the bedrock of the mountain, while the lower terrace, on the outer edge of which the El-Aqsa was built is where the hill slopes most steeply away from the mountain. In consequence, the pavement here is supported on a forest of arches and columns which created the huge underground area that became known as Solomon's stables. During earthquakes the pavement flexes and bends, so much so that the El-Aqsa mosque was destroyed twice within the first century of its building, and has required extensive repair and restoration work ever since.

When Jerusalem fell to the Crusaders in 1099, in a welter of the blood of both Jews and Muslims, the Christian knights naturally took over the Temple Mount along with the rest of the Holy City. Having only the haziest ideas about the history of Jerusalem they believed the mosques were earlier temple buildings appropriated by Muslims. The Dome of the Rock became for them the Temple of the Lord and the El-Aqsa Mosque, which they decided was Solomon's Temple, gave its name to the Order of the Knights Templar who set up their headquarters there.

The short-lived Crusader Kingdom was responsible for some fine rebuilding work in Jerusalem, but on the Haram esh-

Sharif, they fortunately added nothing that ruined either mosque. When Saladin had finally cleared the last of the Christian knights from the Holy Land, both buildings were restored to their former state and have remained as Muslim places of worship ever since, a magnificent testimony to Ummayad architecture and Byzantine mosaic artistry. Fortunately for people of all faiths, or of none, access to the site is now allowed, though for unbelievers it is only at certain times and only through specific gates.

Jews, however, or at least Orthodox ones, are not allowed to set foot there at all. This is not a Muslim edict but a prohibition Orthodox Jews place upon themselves. It seems that the position of the holy of holies – believed by most authorities to be the exposed part of the mountain enshrined beneath the Dome of the Rock – cannot be unquestionably verified. Since only the High Priest was ever allowed to tread the holy of holies, it would be sacrilege for any other Jew to do so, and the whole pavement is therefore a no-go area for them.

All that remains to the Jews is the massive western retaining wall of Herod's pavement, the traditional Wailing Wall, against whose huge eroded blocks they have mourned for the best part of two millenniums over the destruction of their temple. Dressed in the black discarded styles of the nineteenth century ghettos of Eastern Europe, their faces framed by two long, carefully-curled ringlets that fly backwards and forwards like pendulums beneath their wide-brimmed hats, the idiosyncratic figures of Orthodox Jews are no longer the penitential remnant of Judah. Now, as they sway and bob backwards and forwards in front of the pitted wall, they are loudly asserting their right to be there. Occasionally the most militant (and presumably the least orthodox) of them storm the pavement above, reminding Muslims that while they might be in possession of the place at present, Jews are only biding their time: one day soon it will be restored to its rightful owners. Usually major trouble is averted by the patience and forbearance of the sanctuary guardians and a strong police presence.

Until 1967 the Wailing Wall was shut in among narrow streets, and the mourning of religious Jews was a discreet and moving affair. After the Six Day War, however, the entire colourful Quarter of the Moors was wiped out, four hundred families evicted and their houses torn down in order to create a huge open space in front of the Wailing Wall. The wall itself was officially renamed the Western Wall to give it a different flavour. This uncompromising white paved piazza slopes down to the wall like the seating in a Greek theatre, and tourists gather there in large numbers, together with bar mitzvah boys and their families to celebrate and enjoy the spectacle rather than to mourn.

But from where I stood on this bright, crisp morning renewing my acquaintance with a city I loved, I could not see this bizarre modern piazza or the wall. My view stretched outward, beyond the serene golden dome across the Valley of the Kidron, to where the slopes of the Mount of Olives are white with the gravestones of the millenniums. Ascending the slopes, brilliant against the dark green pines and the lighter olives, these acres of the resting places of the dead have a serene and timeless quality. There were Jebusites buried here centuries before the Jews escaped from their bondage in Egypt, and still the bodies come and are laid here in the hope of being first when the ground opens at that final Day of Wrath and Judgement.

The tall bell tower of the Russian compound, the cluster of golden onion domes over the Russian Gethsemane, gold mosaic sparkling from the Latin Gethsemane slightly below, the teardrop outline of the church of Dominus Flevit and, incongruously, above it all, the blinding-white arches of a modern luxury hotel are the punctuation marks on a piece of ground as redolent of the numinous as is the walled city of Jerusalem itself.

And with that thought in mind I left my vantage point to descend by steps across several narrow streets, until I came to the Cardo Maximus, the same main Roman thoroughfare as I had seen depicted in the mosaic map at Madaba only days before. One short section of the Cardo has been excavated, the rest lies beneath the many layers of the city's history. By turning north along the line of this fragment, between the excavated columns, I would come at length to the Christian Quarter and to Holy Sepulchre, which had been summoning me since I entered the city by the Pilgrims Gate the previous afternoon.

Apart from the vast impressive complex of the Haram esh-Sharif, there is nothing in Jerusalem of the splendour of Rome, or Venice or other famous cities of the world. Jerusalem is essentially a small Middle-Eastern town stuck in a time warp. A few of its buildings are rather fine, but all are squashed together within a strictly limited space, cheek by jowl with a jumble of medieval housing, suqs, and winding alleyways; much of it is down at heel. That it is all nonetheless both impressive and deeply moving comes from the associations that almost every one of its stones evokes. For me these associations are Christian and centre around the life, death and resurrection of Jesus of Nazareth.

There has been a worshipping Christian community in Jerusalem since the Day of Pentecost. The very first church of Christ was here. It was made up of his Jewish followers, not just the eleven, but all who had believed in his teaching and on whom the 'Spirit had descended'. It was from this city that the Word went forth to evangelize the world. Stephen, the first martyr, whose face 'was like that of an angel' as he stood up to testify to the new faith, had also walked these streets, and was a member of that first church of Christ. A worshipping community has been maintained in Jerusalem ever since. Small though it might have shrunk at times of greatest persecution, it never entirely died out, and its ranks were continuously swelled by a steady trickle of believers who came to settle in the Holy City.

Because this link with the Jerusalem of Christ remained unbroken, the sites of his Passion, death and resurrection were always honoured and remembered. They were visited regularly and doubtless worship took place there. Knowledge of them was part of the inheritance of the Jerusalem community.

When most of Jerusalem was levelled by Titus after the first century Jewish uprisings, it did not affect the rooted memory of Christians concerning the location of the Holy Places. When Roman Aelia Capitolina rose over the ruins of Jerusalem, the walls of the city also extended further northwards than the previous ones had done. They incorporated the area of the old quarry in which the crucifixion had taken place. Hadrian had the quarry filled in and levelled as a platform for an enormous temple to Aphrodite, which St Jerome claimed was done deliberately in order to destroy a Christian site. But it only succeeded in marking the spot more emphatically. When, two hundred years later, the Empress Helena arrived on her quest to identify the Holy Places, she was able to tap a living tradition.

There seemed to have been no doubt at all about the exact location of both Christ's death and his burial place. Had the Jerusalem Christians placed the sites even a little to the right or left great expense could have been spared. But they were adamant, and Hadrian's temple had first to be torn down and an enormous amount of quarrying work carried out to reveal both the site of the True Cross and the Tomb of Christ. Only after that could a church be raised over the seminal places of Christianity.

As far as authenticity goes it would seem far more difficult to disprove than to prove this site. In any case, since AD 330 Christians world-wide have believed in it implicitly, and millions of pilgrims have come to venerate it, which itself makes for a powerful atmosphere.

The Church of Holy Sepulchre which Constantine built is gone, systematically destroyed by the mad Caliph Hakkim in AD 1009. The building that stands there now is largely Crusader work and really rather fine, but hemmed in on all sides as it is, and only half the extent of the great fourth century atrium and basilica, it is hard not to mourn the loss of the original. The first thing my friend George showed me in Jerusalem years ago was a pastry shop some distance away from Holy Sepulchre, where, tucked away behind doors in a storeroom, a sizeable fragment of a huge pillar and part of the threshold to Constantine's church can still be viewed. It says more than can any diagram or description about the glory that once celebrated the holiest of Christian shrines.

In the centuries since the Crusaders left, Holy Sepulchre has suffered earthquake, fire and vandalism, and is constantly in need of repairs which the three major Christian communities of Jerusalem – Greek, Latin (as the Roman Catholic Church is known here) and Armenian – can seldom agree upon. The church, in consequence, is seldom clear of scaffolding. There are six communities occupying areas of Holy Sepulchre at the present time, but the Syrians, Copts and Ethiopians have had their share of it whittled away over the centuries in the perpetual jockeying for power.

The Ethiopians almost lost their foothold entirely and the monks now live in tiny rough huts on the roof, above Empress Helena's chapel. Here the stumps of elegant springers are all that is left of the vaulting that once supported the roof of the former refectory of the Knights Templar. But this ruined space, open to the stars, where the Ethiopians maintain scraps of gardens around their tiny hovels is the most peaceful spot in the entire church of Holy Sepulchre. Though why anyone should expect to find peace in this place of struggle and death I no longer know. After all, the point was surely that on Easter morning the tomb was found to be empty? This is not 'the garden' but the place of blood and sweat, of the racking of bone and sinew, of the long and bitter agony that was somehow translated into love.

I have grown used to the possessiveness, the jealousies practised here, the attempts by one community to drown out the sounds of others. They are just ripples on the surface and reflect no more than the common failings of human nature. They also say a great deal about the importance in which the shrine is still held and the passions it arouses. That it maintains the power to challenge and inspire is ultimately what matters. I find I mind far more about the ugliness of many of the unnecessary additions imposed on the lovely austere lines of the Crusader building. The perpetual intrusion of cameras and camcorders is also very hard to bear. It is silence that is at a premium in Holy Sepulchre. And yet I believe my feet would find their own way to its doors, so often have they been here. For just occasionally, for no apparent reason, something does break through in Holy Sepulchre which utterly transcends the moment.

Although not a Roman Catholic, when I stay in Jerusalem I

usually attend worship with the Franciscans who are the Latin presence in Holy Sepulchre. This is because I find their celebration the most familiar, and if ecumenism cannot be practised in this city, then the whole idea needs throwing out. On Sundays I go to the Anglican Cathedral of St George which is in East Jerusalem, but to be in the Holy City and not attend daily worship at the central shrine of Christianity would seem perverse. Usually the mass is held at the entrance to the tomb, and different pilgrim groups gather for it each day, Italians, French, Germans, Spaniards all able to follow the service because of the use of the Latin language. The Arab Catholic boys trained by the sisters all sing in slightly harsh throaty voices and I know the service so well now that it is as familiar to me as is the Anglican 1662 prayer book.

Entering Holy Sepulchre from the courtyard through the battered Crusader doorway, the first pause is made just inside where the huge Stone of Unction marks the spot where the body of Christ was laid out for its hasty burial. At Easter the stone runs with oil brought here by devout Greek village women who have saved all their lives to make one pilgrimage to Christ's tomb. Having kissed the stone repeatedly and poured their libation over it, they rub a scarf across the surface to absorb some of the sanctified oil, and this they keep against the day of their own death.

To the right of the stone is a steep narrow flight of steps which leads to Calvary. I could hear the intoning of mass coming from there and made my way up. The small space is divided into two chapels; the Greek one has the stone of the footing of the Cross exposed below the altar where the devout can kneel and touch it. Beaten gold and silver, lace altar cloths, lamps and monstrances all play their part in telling of the unspeakable sorrow in a form made bearable by time and custom.

The Latin side is entirely dominated by a single modern mosaic, the scene of the crucifixion in a bleached landscape. Whether it is a great work of art or not I can never decide, because I have never actually looked at it dispassionately. I always intend to do so but there is something about the place that drives such considerations from my mind. Anglo-Saxon as I am, I never expect to be moved, but I would have to fight very hard not to be so in this place, particularly at this hour before the crowds have had a chance to obscure worship. And the same is true even of the undoubtedly hideous little edicule erected over the tomb of Christ.

Coming out of Holy Sepulchre after mass was to a quite different Jerusalem from the one I had left. It was thronged now with the early morning bustle of people hurrying north and south through the narrow suqs, while stall-holders heaved up the metal shutters of their shops amid a general clattering and clamour. Fruit and vegetable sellers in from the country crouched in corners and against walls with their baskets of produce, while men pushed handcarts through the middle of it, yelling for a clear passage. The supply of goods to the bazaar shops comes mostly by two-wheeled cart, and there is a certain sporting exhilaration about their passage, for where the slopes are steepest, a tyre trailing on a chain behind the cart is jumped upon to act as a brake, and cart and handler go thumping and banging down the steps.

The Via Dolorosa – the Way of the Cross – also winds its way through these narrow suqs, to complete its journey in Holy Sepulchre. A route honoured by devotion rather than history, it begins near St Stephen's Gate and a procession is led along it daily by the Franciscans, while other pilgrims follow it individually or in groups throughout the day, blocking the way as they pause for prayer and worship at the different stations. Except on Fridays, the Muslim day of prayer, when nearly every suq is packed wall to wall with tightly pressed bodies, and it is quicker and more pleasant to make any journey around the outside of the walls, I enjoy weaving my way slowly through this colourful and varied throng. As I had a good hour left before my meeting with George, I thought I would wander slowly to the Damascus Gate where there is a café that serves particularly good Arabic coffee.

The walls of Jerusalem are about two and a half miles in circumference and the irregular sloping rectangle of ground that they enclose not only slopes steeply to the south-east, but also encompasses two shallow valleys, so that the veins and arteries of the city are nearly always ascending or descending and seldom straight for any length, which makes the city seem much larger than it really is. Even the Cardo Maximus whose course I was following, in its present narrow state takes the occasional twist and turn and is certainly not the regal thoroughfare it must have been in Roman times. Only on the final approach to the Damascus Gate are there echoes of an Imperial Roman route, a whisper of the Emperor Hadrian.

The ground rises for the last fifty yards, ascending by way of a flight of broad shallow steps to the present ornate, Ottoman gateway. On the walkway high above, dominating the view, an armed Israeli soldier stood on guard. He lounged there one foot on the parapet, in the bored easy attitude of any soldier in any age looking down casually and slightly curiously on the milling throng of an alien conquered people below him. And there and then it struck home to me, as it had never done before, that not only was this indeed an occupied country, but that there was no essential difference between the Jerusalem of Christ, occupied by the Romans, and this same city occupied now by Israelis.

When I thought about them, the parallels were many and obvious, but the realization that had struck me was at a different level altogether. What it had given me was a sudden brief glimpse into the world in which Christ himself had lived and taught, a world where the political scene was equally as muddied and hopeless as this one.

Everything I had seen so far in my short time in Israel proclaimed openly and unequivocally that this present so-called peace was a sham. The angry journalists had been right, there was not even the semblance of peace. The difference was that now I could face that fact and still believe that there was something of importance and worth for me to discover here.

CHAPTER TWELVE

The Building of a Ghetto

My first Sunday afternoon in the Holy Land found me standing on a hillside just outside Bethlehem, having just escaped from a hard chair and a learned talk in French, which had proved too difficult for me to follow. The previous evening I had attended the midnight service of the Greeks in Holy Sepulchre, which was moving but lengthy. It was still in full swing at 2 a.m. when I had dragged my weary way back to the flat. After only a very few hours sleep I was up again and cycling to St George's Cathedral for the 8 a.m. communion service, followed by my first interview of the day. The natural tendency to overdo things in Jerusalem had caught up with me and it was small wonder that I felt too sleepy to struggle with academic French. Fortunately I would have the opportunity to meet the speaker later on and hear his ideas about the current state of the churches in the Holy Land.

It was in any case far too lovely an afternoon to be cooped up in a close-packed hall. The weather was being particularly kind for January, with a pattern of one day of steady downpour followed by three of bright winter sunshine like today.

From where I was standing the view is immense, with the lovely little hills of Judaea falling away eastward, 'skipping like young rams' down to Jericho and the River Jordan. Beyond the great dramatic slash of the Jordan Valley, the hills of Gilead rise like plumes of smoke in the distance, and the entire scene lies bathed in the wonderful golden light of the Holy Land.

As my gaze wanders back through the middle distance, it comes to rest on a perfect symbol of the land, a grove of olive trees in the middle of what I at first assume to be newly-ploughed fields. But looking more closely, I see that the fields are not ploughed, nor are the trees the symbol of peace, but the still eye in the centre of the whirlwind.

For the second time on this visit I experience the profoundly disturbing sensation that my memory is playing tricks on me. I am not where I thought I was. And yet surely just below this ridge lie the Shepherds' Fields where every Christmas Eve pilgrims from all over the world gather with local Christians to celebrate the appearance of the angel, the great light, and the message of 'Peace on Earth' that accompanied a humble birth in a stable. It is an area of predominantly Christian Palestinian villages that have nestled around Jerusalem since the time of Christ. I remember all this land as lovely terraced fields, olive groves and small stone houses.

But I appear to be standing on the site of some sudden and appalling catastrophe. All around that little clump of olive trees (which for some strange reason has escaped the general destruction) lies devastation. A huge area of ground has been torn apart, trees uprooted, houses reduced to stone rubble. It makes no sense, it is as though a mad army of frenetic beavers has been at work. The mute and ravaged earth is like an enormous open sore with this delicate, chaste beauty at the centre of it.

'But why?' I ask George, who has now joined me and stands grimly surveying the scene. He knows the whole area far better than I do since for years his work has brought him here on a weekly basis, the Armenian Patriarchate having holdings within the Church of the Nativity in Bethlehem as well as in the town itself and the surrounding territory.

'Fifteen years ago,' said George, 'this land was requisitioned by the Israeli authorities. They claimed they were doing it because Jerusalem needed to preserve its green belt, a place from which to contemplate the great beauty of the surrounding landscape. Of course, it already had this, but the Israelis said they feared that if the land was not taken into safekeeping, Palestinians might want to build on it to enlarge their villages. Now the real purpose of the seizure is going into operation; it is to be yet another Israeli settlement, joining up with that one over there.'

The tall white fortress-like structures on the skyline were

behind me and I had not seen them until George pointed them out. Interconnected and uncompromisingly sinister like those going up on the other side of the city, they now appeared doubly charged with menace, as though they were marching on under their own volition. Soon, it is claimed, the circle will close. Instead of a 'green belt' Jerusalem will be entirely enclosed by a ring of these soulless buildings.

The ravaged ground and the 'skipping hills' beyond, many of which skip no longer because of the weight of concrete on them is all occupied territory. More than a third of the hills on the way to Jericho bear their burden of bleak fortress-style apartment blocks where settlers have to be bribed to live, so unsuitable are the surroundings, and so unsociable the way of life. Norman castles served much the same purpose I suppose in the occupation of Britain, only Norman castles were never as ugly as these modern concrete structures. I was reminded of a conversation I had that morning with John Tidy, the English Dean of St George's Cathedral in East Jerusalem. 'It is as though history has been reversed,' he observed. 'Moses stood on Mount Nebo and gazed at the Promised Land and saw a lovely country flowing with milk and honey. Now as the concrete advances, you have to cross the Jordan in the opposite direction to get an echo of the land he saw. It is Jordan that now has the gentle peaceful hills and wooded valleys, the beauty and the peace.' Having just come from those Jordanian hills, I could only echo the sentiment. No matter how many people had talked to me about the land confiscations and the settlements going up, seeing it like this for myself, imposed upon a landscape I knew and loved was a shock, and one which brought the situation home to me far more powerfully than could any words.

Everywhere I had been hearing the same story, that Rabin was buying time with the peace talks, time to build these settlements, to produce a *fait accompli*. Once he had his ring in place, the area of 'Greater Jerusalem' would be one huge ghetto totally separate and independent of the rest of Palestine.

Beit Sahour, the village I had arranged to visit after the lecture is not a stone's throw from where I am standing, and after what I have just been looking at I feel I am in a better position to meet up with some of the people there who have been at the forefront of resistance to Israeli policies in the Occupied Territories. From what I had heard and read of the methods of the villagers of Beit Sahour, I also felt they might have something important to teach the rest of the world about non-violent resistance.

By this time, having been in Israel a week, the background to the current peace talks had become somewhat clearer. The documents and publications I had read, the people I had talked with – Israeli as well as Palestinian, Christians as well as Muslims and Jews, and also foreigners who lived and worked in the land – all led me to the same conclusions.

Looking back over at least the last twenty-eight years, it would appear that no matter which government had been in power, Labour or Likud, doves or hawks, the basic objective in the Occupied Territories had been to push more and more Palestinians out of their country. Since 1967 when Israel occupied all of the West Bank and Gaza this seems to have been achieved largely through continuous harassment allied to intensive land confiscation, especially of the richer more fertile areas. The majority of Palestinians were farmers strongly rooted to the land, and only by breaking that bond could Israel hope to persuade people to leave.

From the first, all water resources were placed under Israeli control, and Palestinian farmers were neither given their rightful share nor allowed to dig fresh wells on their own land. With the lion's share of the water coupled to a foreign-funded modern irrigation system Israeli produce was soon far cheaper than Palestinian. Arab farmers faced with ruin, unable any longer to feed their families were encouraged to take up unskilled menial work, which had the additional bonus of providing Israeli contractors and industrialists with a cheap labour force.

Harassment took the form of heavy punitive taxation, indefinite and arbitrary curfews and other collective civilian punishments, all illegal under international law. By the use of social, economic and psychological pressure the once rich territories were brought to the verge of crisis. An intensive system of arrests was also in operation, together with long periods of administrative detention, particularly designed to break the spirit of the young.

Thousands did leave. When schooling was halted for months at a time, when curfews made visits even to hospital impossible, parents fearing for the futures of their children sought fresh opportunities in other lands. Christians especially, being largely better educated and middle class were more readily accepted into Western countries. From having been around 26 per cent of the population, Christians have now shrunk to rather less than 1 per cent and the possibility of a Holy Land without any Christian presence has become a real possibility.

Finally, those who were left, Muslims and Christians, cried 'Enough' and civil disobedience took over in the form of the *intifada* – a spontaneous movement largely of the young, which meant literally 'We have had enough. We will not be pushed any further.'

Beit Sahour, unique in that 80 per cent of its population has remained Christian, was no different to any other Palestinian town or village in the response of its young to the *intifada*; the children threw stones, and the boys and youths made their Molotov cocktails. Their elders, however, took quite another line. Like the Americans of Boston before them they refused to pay taxes. 'No taxation without representation.' Taxes paid to an occupying power are never in any case felt to be just. The Israeli taxing of Palestinians was typical of an occupying power. They were far higher than for Israelis, and with few if any of the attendant services. Where the authorities were anxious to get their hands on a particular shop or property, the imposition of arbitrarily assessed taxes was often the method used, and tax collection was always accompanied by a heavy military presence. This type of intimidation was one of the main methods used to get so much of the Old City of Jerusalem into Israeli ownership.

At times taxes reached the heights of the absurd – had not the suffering caused by their imposition been so cruel – like the case of all little donkey carts in Gaza being made to carry licence plates.

After the start of the *intifada* the taxation issue became an ever more bitter pill. Palestinians were forced to pay taxes to finance hostile activities against themselves and their brothers in exile. A tax 'for the safety of Galilee' was imposed to finance the invasion of Lebanon, a 'stone tax', to cover the cost of repairing the shattered windscreens of army and settlers' vehicles, an 'absorption tax' to finance the cost of settling new Russian immigrants on land confiscated from Palestinians. There was even a 'Scud tax' for repairing buildings hit by Iraqi missiles in the Gulf War.

When Beit Sahour, population 12,000, decided to raise the banner of tax revolt they did so with their eyes open, fully aware that the tax department had the full weight of the law and the army behind it.

The then Defence Minister, Yitzhak Rabin, took a tough line. 'We are going to teach them a lesson there,' he told the Knesset. 'Even if it takes a month, in the end they will collapse. We will not let this kind of disobedience succeed. We should tell them forget it, even if the curfew on Beit Sahour lasts two months.'

The first assault on Beit Sahour was at 4.30 a.m. on 7 July 1988, when 300 Israeli troops stormed the village, battering down the doors of shops and manhandling the owners into the school yard. Roughly interrogated with a liberal use of force, they were issued with writs ordering them to pay an arbitrary sum within the week. In the meantime their ID cards were confiscated along with their cars.

An ID card is issued to every Palestinian by the occupying authorities and is of paramount significance. It is the one document that proves a Palestinian's right to reside in his own land. Without it he is automatically assumed to be an illegal immigrant and can in theory be instantly deported to become a stateless refugee. Every Palestinian dreads the possibility of losing his ID card. He guards it with his life, and yet it is also the means of his constant humiliation. Israeli soldiers use the threat of confiscating or tearing up the ID card in order to impose on the spot tasks, like helping to dismantle a road block, haul down a Palestinian flag from a telegraph pole, clean graffiti off a wall, or just to provide passing amusement for bored soldiers. Already during my present visit I had witnessed this type of the abuse of authority by soldiers misusing ID cards at checkpoints, one more depressingly reminiscent example of the way Romans had behaved in this land when their Empire held sway.

When the rest of the citizens of Beit Sahour got wind of the ID confiscations, many of them gathered in front of the town hall; leading citizens, clergy, teachers, heads of local institutes and ordinary citizens. All of them handed in their ID cards with the request that they be given back to the issuing authority as they no longer accepted that authority's right to issue them. This action together with the burning of the tax bills seriously threatened to undermine Israeli authority. No wonder Rabin took it seriously. Had other towns in the Occupied Territories found the courage to follow suit peace might well have been a reality by now.

The reprisals that followed Beit Sahour's stand took many forms, and cannot be said to have fully ended yet. Threats of deportations, long curfews, seizure of goods, an army presence on the rooftops at hundred metre intervals to ensure no food or medical supplies entered the town. Telephone lines were cut, journalists forbidden entry. The whole town and surrounding area was declared a military no-go zone. Even a delegation of high-ranking church officials wanting to come and pray with the imprisoned town people, and a diplomatic mission from Sweden were not permitted entry. Israeli citizens who felt sympathy with the Palestinian cause and had already begun to have regular talks at the Rapprochement Centre were also denied access to the town.

The sort of curfews imposed in the Occupied Territories were in reality often a total siege where no one, man, woman or child, was permitted to set foot outside their door for any purpose whatsoever. Those who try to do so are arrested or shot. It is a very severe punishment and a most effective method of subduing a subject people. Added to the isolation, the deprivation of normal social intercourse, is the acute frustration and boredom. No one can go to work, tend their fields or their animals. Children can't go to school. Food and medicine cannot be renewed. If something goes wrong with water, electricity or the like no one can be summoned to repair it. During a curfew there are inevitable tragedies. The first curfew imposed on Beit Sahour lasted eleven days and was the first of many. There were deaths, innumerable severe beatings and broken bones; there was a spate of arrests and long periods of administrative detention in the notorious desert prisons.

There were also punitive raids where the tax-collectors, aided by the army, stripped shops, factories and stores and even homes of goods and chattels. Pharmacies were emptied of their entire stocks which were then left in the hot sun until the drugs were spoiled and useless. People's refrigerators and televisions were taken, even children's toys were seized, thrown roughly onto lorries and driven off, ostensibly to be sold to pay the taxes.

Every household also received a leaflet extolling the advantages of emigrating to America, and offering cash incentives to do so, though the bureau responsible for their circulation was never identified.

That Beit Sahour was able to survive and not capitulate was largely due to its system of neighbourhood committees which could organize the individual efforts of the community and keep things going even under curfew. Beit Sahour had plenty of experts in many fields and had prepared itself for the conflict. It had its own backyard gardens of vegetables, chickens and rabbits, and no one went hungry even during the worst sieges. It could organize its own health systems, its own schools, street cleaning and the like. But even these non-political committees were eventually declared illegal, and membership of them made punishable by a long term of imprisonment.

What finally won the day was the moral strength of the people of Beit Sahour who, no matter what the provocation, resolutely refused to fall into the trap of hating their enemy. By persevering in their fight for justice, peace and reconciliation through non-violent means, they earned for themselves friends and supporters throughout the world. It was American Jews who offered to bear the cost of replacing what had been destroyed or seized by Israel in the tax raids. It also led to a wider world awareness of what was really going on in the Occupied Territories, and must to some extent have added to the onset of the current peace talks. The village was recommended for a Nobel Peace Prize.

It was Beit Sahour's own peace talks still continuing at the Rapprochement Centre that were the main reason for my being there. Communication between Jerusalem and the Occupied Territories is extremely difficult since hardly anyone living in the Occupied Territories is allowed to travel in or across Israel. Even where it is occupied Palestinian territory, like East Jerusalem and the Old City itself, some law is made up to exclude Palestinian entry. This means there are Palestinians in responsible, highly-skilled jobs who have to risk their freedom daily by travelling to work illegally. It also means that any foreigner who wants to meet a particular Palestinian has to be prepared to travel out to him or her. At least foreigners can still move freely in most areas.

The person I found manning the office was a young man I shall call Simon. After giving me the information I wanted and telling me the dates and times of meetings, he took me home to drink tea and to meet his family. He was very conscious of his roots. His house was built over the sort of natural caves that abound in the area and once provided shelter for a pastoral people and their animals; such a place as might well have sheltered the Christ Child's birth. Simon's story was typical of many I would hear in the next few weeks.

'When the soldiers come to arrest you, you realize at once how frightened they are. They leave their armoured cars down the hill and a squad of about thirty soldiers come up silently. They kick in the back door and the front door at the same time if they can, and they call you: "Simon get up, we have come for you." They know all the names. Sometimes I was surprised. I think it is me they have come for and they call one of my brothers; sometimes it is the other way round. They get the handcuffs on you and they beat you while they rush you down the hill to the car. And again in the car they beat you.'

'Were you terrified?' I ask.

'No, all the boys knew what they had to do, which is not to cry, not to groan, not to fall down. You laugh if you can, and you take everything they do to you without giving in. Resistance is everything. I think the first time really you were relieved that at last it was happening to you and you can bear it.'

Simon was arrested six times during the *intifada* and always sentenced under administrative detention. Never once did he have a trial. The offence was always stone-throwing, except for a single occasion when it had been a 'cocktail Molotov' (*sic*). On his first arrest he was tortured for forty-eight days – the eighteen days questioning allowed by Israeli law, followed immediately by a thirty-day extension, also sanctioned by law. He was seventeen years old. It was winter and freezing cold at nights (as I well knew). He was wearing only a shirt and trousers and was kept in what he described as a sort of windowless outhouse. A stinking sack was over his head.

'I was glad of the sack, it helped to keep me warm. I was handcuffed to a chair and not allowed to sleep for the first eighteen days. The guard kicked the chair every time my head dropped. Sometimes I was stood bent over with the handcuffs fastened to the wall high up behind me so every bit of my body was straining. When they took me for questioning, they kept my hands handcuffed behind my back and pulled me along by the hood like a donkey (he shows me how they did this first, tightening and bunching the sack under his chin so that his face is jerked upward and forward). They always made me walk a sort of obstacle course so that I kept stumbling and falling.'

I ask him what the questioning was about, and he tells me it is to have names. 'They know all the names, but they want you to say them. If you betray your friends, your spirit is broken. You are nothing any more.'

I ask him how they had tortured him, and he tells me it was by hitting him, not hard, but on exactly the same spot, maybe a breastbone, for hours at a time. It leaves no mark, but he tells me there are places on his body which still ache from this treatment. He doesn't volunteer further details and I don't press him.

Instead he goes on to talk about prison, which in his case was Ansar 111, deep in the Negev Desert. The desert prisons are simply constructed, essentially square pits in the sand surrounded by high walls along which armoured cars can patrol. Each pit is separated from the others by similar walls and each holds about two hundred men in tented accommodation, twenty-six to a tent. The desert sun beats down remorselessly on guards and prisoners alike.

'It was a privilege to be there,' said Simon. 'I would wake up at Ansar thinking, Thank God I am here now, I have nothing further to fear. But first comes adjustment which is a necessity if you are to survive.'

He said he made himself give up all thoughts of life outside, and concentrated on the idea that this was the chance to get to know himself, and to build a new personality. A year was the longest time he served, though on release he was immediately re-arrested and served a further eight months. He did not keep a calendar to tick off the days, but instead tried just to live each day as it came. 'You live so closely with the other prisoners, you had to work very hard to maintain respect and liking for one another.' This he felt kept you brave and resistant and was to prove very counter-productive for the Israelis.

Eventually he gave up active resistance, stone-throwing and the like, not because of the consequences – he would have been treated in the same way by the Israelis whether he had been guilty or not he felt – but simply because he had grown beyond that type of activity. The Israelis had tried to break him and they had failed. In the process he realized he had become far stronger than his persecutors. He had also become a far better Christian than I felt I could ever hope to be, for in spite of everything that had been done to him, he seemed to bear absolutely no ill will towards any man.

CHAPTER THIRTEEN

Gaza

Gaza is not a name to conjure up pleasant expectations, but it was somewhere I knew I had to see for myself. It was not the easiest place to get to at present, for without actually declaring it a no-go zone, Israel was not encouraging foreigners into the area. Several companies who organized tours of the Gaza refugee camps as part of a Holy Land visit were now officially prevented from doing so, and even individuals could be held up indefinitely at the checkpoint. There was also the possibility that without proper introductions I might well encounter suspicion from the Palestinians themselves, which would take time and patience to overcome; time I did not have. I therefore jumped at the opportunity of going there with Bill Warnock, who ran the World Vision organization in Israel and who had several projects going in Gaza which he visited once or twice a month.

There could be no doubting Bill's nationality. The rubbery features – usually stretched in an engaging grin – the long loose-limbed body and the earnest forthright handshake marked him unmistakably. He also had a habit of dropping names about with the casualness of someone scattering confetti – 'Last time I was speaking to Bill Clinton . . .' – that was not to be taken too seriously. Every new acquaintance, including myself, was instantly endowed with heightened status that was disarming as well as amusing. For an aid agency that relies on attracting funds from many different sources Bill was obviously an asset, but what I came to appreciate most about him was his honest outspokenness. He does not like what is happening in Israel and is not reluctant to say so. He thinks neither Israel nor the US are serious about peace, and that the White House itself is becoming Zionized.

We set off for Gaza early one morning and as Bill lived just outside the huge checkpoint to the north of the city I rode over to his place by bicycle to avoid him having to run through the security process twice. Everyone who spends any time in Israel tries to avoid these checkpoints which can be pointlessly confrontational as well as time-wasting. This one on the road to Ramallah was new to me, a large, high profile affair, and very unpleasant with its mixture of rough utilitarian squalor and military might. It had turned an attractive middle-class Palestinian suburb into something resembling a wasteland. I dispensed with the need for a soldier to check my identity by simply taking to the pavement, where I passed unnoticed. When all one's Palestinian friends are being subjected to daily harassment these small rather juvenile triumphs afford a certain satisfaction.

Bill was waiting with his large luxurious car and after securing Roberts in his house we set off through the lovely ter-raced hills of a gentle countryside which I could remember bicycling through in previous years at a considerably more leisured pace. This part of Israel is all pastoral land, lovingly tended by Palestinian farmers for thousands of years. But here too the sharp-edged concrete settlements now make their incongruous, aggressive appearance pressing in upon the vine-yards and the terraced fields.

Bill's employer, World Vision, is a Christian relief and devel-opment organization which works in many different countries. In Israel its brief is to foster peace and reconciliation and its par-ticular role is to identify special need among the Palestinians, both Muslims and Christians, of the Occupied Territories. It funds small-scale projects in the field of education and eco-nomic self-help – a library for a college, or help with setting up a bakery or a bee-keeping scheme. Several villages that had ben-efited from this sort of aid were pointed out to me as we drove past, and usually there would be a Jewish settlement butting up hard against them.

In the area of Latrun, among the terraced vines and olive groves we encountered a different discordant note, where stiff foreign-looking conifers had been planted to make an area called Canada Park. It had been created on the ruins of three Arab villages, whose destruction had been ordered by Yitzhak Rabin in 1967 when he was Chief of Staff. Nine thousand Palestinians were forced from their homes at gunpoint in this expulsion which even the Israeli army had questioned. What I had not known until Bill told me, was that one of those villages was a possible site of the elusive biblical Emmaus, where the Risen Christ was recognized in the breaking of the bread.

The significance of Emmaus, which is surely the beginning and the ending of all journeys made us both fall silent while the powerful car purred on, carrying us down to the coastal plain.

The misery of Gaza reaches out beyond the wide perimeter no man's land of the checkpoint. The bleak high fencing, the coils of razor wire and the wide, flat scene of desolation spelling misery and poverty were all reminiscent of films shot in Poland and Austria in the early years of World War II, only then it had been Jews behind the wire and the soldiers of the Third Reich who were manning the watch-towers and wielding the guns.

The crossing itself was terrifying, with checkpoint after checkpoint, all manned by bored or aggressive, sloppily-dressed soldiers who, considering they were handling such lethal weaponry, were frighteningly casual in their attitude. Back-up posts, heavy guns, watch-towers, loudspeakers, arc lights – all the paraphernalia of military control – surrounded us in this horrible stretch of oil-soaked, debased earth.

As everyone who has had experience of this and other Israeli crossing points is aware, it is the carelessness of the guards that constitutes the greatest danger; one soldier will wave you through while his companion cries halt. To go on will certainly mean a burst of automatic fire, to stay could provoke the same reaction. The need for constant vigilance is very wearing. Bill however was an old hand and a natural dealer. With the broadest of American drawls and the vaguest of explanations, as well as an arrogance to equal that with which we were confronted, he had us through the succession of checkpoints and around to the back door or 'industrial' approach in a matter of minutes. One of the many indefinite curfews was in force at the time in response to the suicide bombing of a bus in Tel Aviv. It was to continue for several weeks and was still in operation when I left Israel.

There seems to be no pretence on the part of Israel that these curfews serve any useful purpose in containing the situation, or in preventing acts of terrorism by Muslim extremists. They are intended simply as a means of inflicting corporate punishment on a civilian population. Such umbrella curfews totally contravene the international laws to which Israel is a signatory. They cause great hardship and untold suffering and, as many authorities have pointed out, they exacerbate the Palestinians' frustration and despair to the point where strapping a bomb to one's own body and setting out on a suicide killing mission becomes more rather than less probable. By the imposition of curfews and draconian travel restrictions, Gaza and the West Bank have, in effect, been turned into vast ghettos.

Present-day Gaza is a long, thin fertile strip of land beside the Mediterranean Sea, an area once renowned for its orange groves and rich farmland. Gaza City in the north of the region has a few Christian churches that have long existed in harmony with their Muslim neighbours, as is usually the case in Palestine. A number of very fine houses grace the esplanades, otherwise, until 1948 changed the face of Palestine, the strip was predominantly pastoral with small scattered villages and a population numbering around a hundred thousand.

After 1948 when the State of Israel was declared amid furious fighting on both sides, wave after wave of refugees fled here, most of whom were settled in camps. The population is now well over a million, a half of which is under sixteen years of age. To add to the impossible overcrowding, Israel has confiscated just over 40 per cent of the Gaza Strip for Jewish settlements, and appropriated 80 per cent of the water supply. The Jewish settlements use only a fraction of this precious commodity; the rest is piped out into various Israeli irrigation schemes in the neighbouring Negev Desert. Visitors who exclaim with delight over the greening of the desert little realize the cost involved in human misery. What remains of Gaza's water has to serve the vastly swollen Palestinian population and is recycled again and again until it is dangerously in excess of the UN levels for nitrates and other toxic chemicals.

But all these facts and a hundred like them can be read dry-eyed. Encountering the human degradation they represent is a different matter.

Among the sheaths of razor wire, the mud and the litter, where a torn piece of fencing could be pushed aside we entered the area of newly-established 'limited' Palestinian autonomy. Bill parked our car and we were ushered over to a much rougher vehicle which had Gazan registration plates and which was driven by Bill's Palestinian helper, Yassir. Bill has been trying for well over a year to get this young man a pass to enable him to come to Jerusalem for meetings and day-training but without success. No reason is given for the refusal, and it means hours and hours of Bill's time is wasted having to come and deal with everything personally.

The muddy trampled space where we had entered was full of people waiting hopelessly for passes to travel to other parts of the Occupied Territories. Some were special cases, awaiting permission to attend hospital or a funeral or visit a sick family member. Most had already been waiting for hours. Some who had been granted passes were now waiting on the whim of the soldiers who manned the wire to let them through; many of these had also been waiting for hours.

The system for people like Yassir needing a pass to make regular journeys, perhaps to work, to university, or for training courses, can take months, or even years of applying and re-applying and even then achieve nothing. Everyone has to turn up in person to see if his or her application has been granted, and the reports of the high level of gratuitous cruelty and harassment at these sessions are too consistent to dismiss; they make disturbing reading. Israeli female army personnel are usually in charge and one favourite ploy is to call the applicant by name and say 'Congratulations, Mr So-and-so, your application has been turned down.' Another is to drop the card when handing it over and then simulate anger at the 'abuse' of Israeli property. As the person bends down to retrieve the card a knee smashes into his face. This is also a frequent ploy with ID cards at checkpoints. Wealthy Gazan families with sophisticated children educated in the States are treated no differently. Mothers of such families confess their fear of sons snapping under such treatment, and reacting in a way that will result in their being shot on the spot or permanently maimed. Plastic surgery to remedy facial injuries is one of Gaza's greatest needs.

Restriction of movement seriously affects the Gazan economy; the extended curfew system even more so, and both have added to the desperate poverty that now afflicts Gaza. It runs on a shoe-string economy, and when teachers can't get to their schools, folk can't get to work, supplies can't get in, the complex business of daily life breaks down and what little people have is wasted.

Bill and I, stepping past the razor wire littered with a thousand bits of blown detritus, were aliens from another world. What did we know of ghetto life? How could anyone who has not lived like this appreciate the thousand and one pinpricks; the endless difficulties and complications, large and small, that grind one down, all multiplied and blown out of proportion by a terrifyingly punitive bureaucracy operating outside the wire? Even from the perimeter I was in a sweat of claustrophobia, but at least I knew I could turn and run whenever I chose.

Jabalia Camp was far worse. As we drove through its streets I thought that if the rest of the caring world could have just half an hour here, support for Israel's position would collapse instantly. Possibly Israel realizes this too, which is why visits here are made so difficult. One line from Shakespeare's *Henry the Fifth* rang through my head all day. It is when at the Battle of Agincourt the King finds that French soldiers have wantonly slain the unarmed young boys among the baggage train – 'I was not angry since I came to France, until this instant.' I too was angry, sick with it. I cannot see how anyone can visit Jabalia Camp and not be angry. The shock of seeing it was similar to what I had felt as a child of eleven when, after World War II, the pictures and the first-hand accounts of Nazi atrocities began to fill the pages of the newspapers. The sense of impotence, shame and anger that I felt then I now realize comes from a simple acceptance of a shared humanity. In the words of Christ, 'Inasmuch as you do it unto these the least of my brethren you do it unto me.'

Conditions were appalling. We drove through lakes of sewage, between housing that was shacks cobbled together with disparate scrap materials, while little children, the third generation of refugees who had been forced to live here, picked a cautious, painful route on bare feet through the ravaged littered ground that passed for streets. The dust and dirt were terrible causing all sorts of eye infections and health problems. I found it all far worse than refugee camps I had visited in Africa and the poorer parts of India, mainly because civilization had advanced so much further here that the destruction of it made for a greater degradation. Nor was it drought or any natural calamity that had brought about these conditions but the deliberate policy of an occupying force.

I could see little difference in principle between the thieving of property, the disregard of life and rights that had been practised on the Jews of Europe by the Nazi regime, and what Israeli Jews themselves had done and were continuing to do here to a people whose land they had taken and occupied and whose livelihoods they had wrecked.

The streets of Jabalia merged into the outskirts of Gaza City where the same breakdown of the infrastructure was apparent everywhere. There was even a football field about a foot deep in sewage and debris. At the Isolation Hospital the sewage had begun to seep up through the floorboards, but here at least outside aid had got to work and a new complex of septic tanks was nearing completion. One of the volunteer engineers working on this scheme came from a former Eastern bloc country. 'In my country we know something about oppression, which is why I am here to help,' he told me, pointing out another Jewish settlement on nearby high ground, whose sewage discharge would apparently constitute a further threat to the Palestinian hospital.

We had visits to make to all sorts of small-scale aid schemes funded by World Vision. One was a club for children with abnormal behaviour, where structured play was used as therapy. Trauma is unnaturally high in a society where scarcely a family is without at least one member in prison, and where death, injury and beatings inflicted by soldiers have been a part of everyday life. That Rabin's instruction to the Israeli army to break the bones of children caught throwing stones was made quite openly without fear of international censure should give us pause. Palestinian adults are equally traumatized by conditions and this often results in them beating their children, thus adding to the level of behavioural difficulties.

Now that limited self-rule has begun, everyone agrees that an oppressive weight has been lifted off Gaza simply by the absence of Israeli soldiers patrolling the streets. But the scars inflicted by a heavy, confrontational military presence are still very fresh, and since material conditions have not improved at all, the difference is not as great as it might be.

It is one thing to be granted a degree of autonomy but without funds to administer it, what does it amount to? It leads to the question of whether it is an inevitable failure of the new Palestinian administration for which Israel hopes. One little boy playing at the centre made us aware of a fresh difficulty, for he was equally fearful of Arafat's police force who are dressed almost identically to the Israeli soldiers. For this child the terror was still present.

We visited a Palestinian family in one of the Gaza camps who had just been rehoused through international aid in a simple single-roomed structure. Amongst so much desperate need this case had been singled out; many are in a similar plight but there is just not aid enough to go around. The family had six children and no visible means of support. The oldest child was about twelve and the youngest still a baby. Most of them had wracking coughs and were clearly in need of the clothes we had brought them. But somehow in the one room an impressive level of cleanliness had been maintained and the older children were eager and intelligent looking. One doe-eyed boy of ten lay on the floor on a mattress, permanently paralysed, having been shot in the spine by an Israeli soldier when he was climbing onto a building to fly a Palestinian flag from the roof. The family are very proud of this little victim of gratuitous savagery, and refer to him as their 'martyr'. One of the few acts of resistance left to these people is to breed children to become 'martyrs' to the Palestinian cause and most families proudly display photographs of their dead or imprisoned sons.

Unemployment is reckoned at 90 per cent in Gaza and it gets worse with each closing of the checkpoints which is accompanied by further importation of foreign labour to replace the Palestinians. No jobs, no present, no hope of a future, what remains but anger and despair?

And yet this terrible place is also a triumph of the human spirit. Even the degree of normality which is maintained under such conditions is in itself wonderful. With no money, no budget, no salaries, there were so many people, Muslims and Christians working together to tackle the problems of the wider community, not only with commitment but with love. And love and commitment had often to suffice, because supplies were so scarce and the training of personnel was so often disrupted by the closures of the territories.

In the streets, at even the humblest level, there was a creativity that came from having to make do. They might lack shoes but the children were as clean and as tidy as the contaminated water could make them. Where there were schools they were taught. A certain black humour was pressed into service to keep despair at bay, and of the majority I would say the spirit was certainly not broken.

We saw schools for the deaf operating in shacks where, with a minimum of anything other than goodwill, small Muslim children were breaking out of their cocoon of isolation and beginning to communicate. How much more could have been done with an adequacy of materials and fully-trained teachers was clear, but the dedication was something very special. These teachers, both Muslim and Christian reminded me of the passage in Acts about Stephen's face 'shining like an angel'. They too shone; and because of them Gaza was bearable.

I also met several of the impressive people who were responsible for Gaza functioning at all. Surgeons, doctors, specialists of all kinds, they could have been enjoying a comfortable life in any of a score of Western countries, where their skills would have had free rein. Many of them had indeed done so, but after years, often in very high positions, had returned, drawn back by their ties with the land and by a sense of identity with their fellow Palestinians. These able people, again both Muslims and Christians, worked tirelessly, filling frustrating but necessary roles in Gaza, like keeping some sort of health care operating, getting emergency cases to hospitals in Jerusalem through the maze of restrictive bureaucracy; administering all the many and complicated strands of aid and relief, with hands that were desperately empty of funding.

The selfless workers of Gaza reminded me of the way the early Celtic Church had recognized two forms of martyrdom, the red and the white. Red martyrdom meant dying or being killed for your faith, and that is a concept that is much in vogue here, though debased I think by modern usage. Courageous they might be, but I cannot accept that soldiers killed in battle, children wounded in ugly skirmishes, or terrorists sacrificing their lives to kill others are martyrs. Surely the majority of them are simply the victims of the cruelty of others or of their own mistaken ideas.

White martyrdom on the other hand required a person to live for his or her faith by daily sacrifice. It was nothing less than a total service to God and to one's fellow men – a 'slow dying of the self to love' – and of this quality there is an abundance in Gaza. Small wonder that I was able to come away from the place with this sense of people's faces literally shining.

But this comfort took some time to supplant the anger I felt at what man's inhumanity had done in Gaza. It was anger that saw me through the tedious three hours Bill and I spent at the checkpoint before we could leave after that first visit. Half-way through the afternoon, Bill had learnt from the hospital administrator that a consignment of much needed drugs and equipment which World Vision had shipped over from the States had been unaccountably held up. Messages concerning it had been winging to and fro all day on portable telephones, but now apparently stalemate had been reached and the two containers were about to disappear into limbo.

Yassir rushed us back from the work of the clinics to the horrible border control area, fuelling my anger on the way with glimpses of vast acres of lush green land behind high security fencing where Israeli settlements flourished on land so desperately needed by its rightful owners.

We learned that the two containers, which had already been cleared at all levels, had made it to the third or fourth halt of the checkpoint where a soldier had arbitrarily decided it should go no further. 'There's a curfew isn't there, so why should we let this in?' Bill of course knew a useful person or two in the upper echelons of the Israeli Administration, and more importantly could produce one on the end of a telephone line. With a lot of bluff on Bill's part, and face-saving on the Israeli side, things were put in motion, containers located, the transporters traced and recalled.

Since I had no part to play in these rounds of tense telephoning and impassioned confrontations with army personnel, I was free to study the surroundings and the actions of the soldiers. It was at this point that I began to see that they too were victims. Each and every Israeli, male and female is called upon to do military training, and when that initial period is finished, a few weeks every year is spent back in uniform. You cannot serve in an army of occupation without being affected by it. The fear of patrolling the streets of Gaza with the constant threat of ambush from a thousand places is bad enough, but to be party to breaking the bones of children, to shooting and gassing unarmed civilians, to demolishing people's houses simply because a relation has been found guilty of terrorism or on some minor legal quibble are corrupting experiences. The question becomes who is the most deeply traumatized, victim or perpetrator?

One game the soldiers played to ease the monotony was making lorries drive fast over speed humps. The loudspeakers would blare out from the tall watch-tower at the approaching vehicle 'Hurry, hurry, hurry' and as it gathered speed and hurtled towards the axle-breaking hump I wondered whether they were laying bets on the outcome.

The loudspeakers harried us too as we went from place to

place tracking our missing containers. Childishly perhaps we got our own back through role-play. I became an American journalist accompanying the consignment and writing a piece about it for the people back home. 'How long has it been held up so far?' I would ask Bill, writing busily in my notebook. 'Twelve hours? Gosh! Well it makes a real powerful story, and every hour we wait it gets better.' 'Yes,' agrees Bill, 'it certainly shows what things are like here.' 'So who cares?' said the sergeant, understandably nettled by all this. 'You do,' I said, taking my cue. 'This gift to the people of Gaza comes from the people of America, the very people who put the bread in your stomachs.' And here, carried away by the part, I poked him in his own ample middle to add weight to my words. As this is a gesture common among Israelis he did not take offence, it even lightened the atmosphere a little. Several other soldiers gathered round to listen; any diversion made a welcome break.

Bill and I changed tack and started complaining about the squalor and ugliness of this awful border checkpoint, and the monstrous mess that Israel had made of Gaza. The soldiers said it was nothing to do with them, it was the Gazans' responsibility. That argument was easily demolished, and for a moment it seemed we almost had a platform for meaningful discussion. One soldier said he would much rather be at home than manning this post, and then fell silent when we pointed out that it was he who was wielding the gun, not us or the Gazans.

At this point higher authority intervened with the news that our retrieved containers were now all ready to roll on into Gaza – perhaps the process had been accelerated by someone getting worried over the success of our private peace talks. The consignment was Yassir's responsibility now, and Bill and I were free to return to the comparative comfort of what seemed like another world. As we made our farewells the western sky over Gaza was already darkening with banks of black and purple clouds. Exhausted and drained of all emotion we drove in silence back to Jerusalem.

CHAPTER FOURTEEN

Where is the Peace?

The most perfect example of Crusader architecture in Jerusalem is the church of St Anne, a building whose austere lines and perfect proportions have been left uncluttered and free of all but the simplest furnishings. It stands in the Muslim Quarter, near St Stephen's Gate, on an unusually spacious site, much of which is taken up by the romantic ruins of a much larger Byzantine church that was yet another casualty of the mad Caliph Hakkim. Since it offers one of the most peaceful havens in Jerusalem, I go there often.

The Byzantines celebrated the site as the birthplace of the Virgin Mary, hence the dedication, but it also had other important associations. The ruins cover a large cistern that in Roman times was the Pool of Bethesda where Jesus healed the paralysed man who was never able to get into the pool at the curative moment when 'the waters moved'. Excavations have revealed that the mysterious turbulence in the pool was caused by the fact that several cisterns, including the one serving Herod's temple were interconnected and a natural syphoning action took place when the water reached a certain level. Belief in the miraculous properties of the pool had tradition to feed upon, since previously the site had been a centre of healing of the cult of Asclepias, remains of which have also been excavated and are on display together with the cisterns. Traditions connected with such places live on, contributing perhaps even to the sense of peace to be found there today.

On this occasion, however, I was at St Anne's to meet one of the White Fathers whose order had been given charge of the site when the Ottomans had handed it over to France. An impressive scholar, Father Bouwen had spent several decades in the Holy Land and had his finger on the pulse of life in Jerusalem. I had met him on previous visits and valued his insights. Having given up on his lecture at Bethlehem, I would now be able to hear his views expressed in his admirable English.

I was early for my appointment, and while I waited, reading over my notes in the garden, I was inundated by a large party of Japanese tourists who swept over me with the inexorability of a tidal wave. They were clutching cameras as they ran, so that for a moment I thought I was missing out on some world-shattering event which they were desperate to record. But I soon saw it was merely the tightness of their schedule that was driving them. Pausing momentarily, like a wave before it topples, they checked the direction of the low afternoon sun, before taking up positions in groups around the ruins.

Shutters snapping like castanets, person after person ran out from each group to take his or her picture and immediately ran back to be included in the next shot, while another took their place. When all had their record of this particular stop on their Holy Land itinerary, they were off again through the gate as though sucked out by the action of a particularly strong undertow. Apart from the familiar faces of their companions I don't think they could have registered anything of this lovely place.

Father Bouwen wisely waited for the tide to depart before appearing to escort me to his study. A spare, ageless looking man with a scholar's pale and serious features, his face lit up in a rare smile as he told me about the initial euphoria that greeted the Peace Accord. He said he would never forget September 1993 when the announcement was made. The streets which had been so empty throughout the *intifada* were suddenly full; the whole Quarter – families, children, dancing, celebrating, waving flags – it was like the end of the war in Europe. Now, more than a year later, nothing had happened and it had all turned sour. He doubted whether there is even enough accord between the Jewish leaders for any meaningful peace to advance. Peres had his vision of peaceful co-existence, while Rabin saw a complete separation of the two peoples and placed the emphasis upon maximum security. Double standards applied everywhere at all levels. Until Israelis could stop seeing the whole world against them and themselves as different in kind; until they could develop the ability to put themselves in another's shoes, there was not much hope. He thought they did not even realize the effort President Sadat of Egypt had made in coming to Israel on that historic occasion.

Father Bouwen seemed to be saying, as were many others, that conditions were worse now than they had been before the Peace Accord. The *intifada* had brought people together, forced co-operation. It had even made common ground among the clergy of the various churches, usually so much more intent on defending their privileges. The churches had worked together to alleviate suffering. But now that the *intifada* had been replaced by a peace that was no peace – no prisoners released, no changes in people's circumstances, settlements going up all around Jerusalem, it felt like a betrayal. Poverty in Jerusalem was growing at an alarming rate. Rejoicing had been replaced by the slow death of hope.

Nor did any other Jerusalem people I talked to, clergy or laity, Christian, Muslim or Jew, offer me a more optimistic scenario. Jews were difficult to meet in any case. The Jews encountered in the Old City were mostly settlers, many newly arrived, heavily armed and highly confrontational – like the crowds seen on the world's screens celebrating Goldstein's massacre of the Muslims at prayer in the mosque at Hebron. These settlers are heavily subsidized, a part of Rabin's policy, it is believed, for hastening the colonization of Arab Jerusalem and squeezing out the Palestinians.

They advertise their presence as though it were a military conquest, draping enormous Israeli flags over the front of every building or apartment they acquire. The widely-condemned former Defence Minister, Ariel Sharon, procured a particularly conspicuous home in the heart of the Muslim Quarter. It is permanently guarded by soldiers in flak jackets, and it sports a blue and white Israeli banner twenty feet long over an arch beneath which every Muslim going to pray at the El-Aqsa mosque must pass. Any means are used for Jews to gain a foothold in the

Muslim and Christian Quarters, but even the Armenian Quarter now has its Jewish settlers who resolutely refuse to exchange even a 'good morning' with their Christian neighbours. There is no shortage of money for the purpose of Jews buying property in the Old City but even so some buildings, like the St John's Hospice close to Holy Sepulchre, are seized illegally and occupied, and there seems to be no effective way of evicting Jewish squatters.

Jerusalem housing is medieval and full of surprises. I knock at doors in dark narrow alleyways and friends lead me up crooked flights of steps, through several levels, to emerge finally into sunlight high above the deeply-shadowed suqs. From these unexpected rooftop gardens with their vines and fruit trees the Golden Dome shimmers before me through thickets of television aerials, closer than I would have thought possible. It is a simpler, more intimate world at this level: one shared with the Jerusalem sparrows who make their homes among the domes and spires.

For Muslim and Christian children, this area was once a playground. They could cross from garden to garden to the wide areas of the roofed over markets and cisterns and need never touch ground. But now every individual garden has become an embattled area with a high barbed wire fence around it for fear of the settlers, who will trample through anyone's property with impunity since they are the only people in the city, apart from the soldiers, who are armed. Women alone in their houses, or minding young children, are terrified on being suddenly confronted in their own homes by these aggressive, heavily-bearded, gun-toting men. Their nights are further disturbed by the strange shrieks and cries coming from a nearby yeshiva, which was set up especially for reformed Jewish criminals.

From the roof garden of my friend, Maya's house, I can see from the plethora of Israeli flags how great has been the encroachment of Jewish settlers into the Muslim Quarter. Just a few yards away on a separate roof there is even a makeshift gun emplacement from which the whole area can be raked. It is all very high-profile and threatening, and it seems clear that as a planned demographic policy it is working. The people of Jerusalem, both Christian and Muslim are intimidated; they feel they are under siege. The most able of them continue to leave for a better life elsewhere, and this further impoverishes the besieged communities. It makes the impossible believable – that soon there might be no more Christians in Jerusalem.

Another innovation since my last visit has been the installation of strong metal grills to cover the courtyards in the Muslim Quarter. These were necessary because of the metal bars and other missiles which rained down on Muslim families, thrown from the windows of upper apartments which had been taken over by Jewish settlers, or from the roofs of the new yeshivas set up in the quarter. It is claimed that Arab children were deliberately targeted. The town council, however, did nothing to protect its Arab citizens, and it was left to the religious authority of the Haram esh-Sharif to fit the grills, the tops of which I could see were already littered with iron bars and other missiles.

I find it difficult to believe that any adult can feel such hatred towards children of another race that they would deliberately attempt to kill or maim them. Even when I see Jewish settlers actually spitting at small Arab boys as they pass them in the street I cannot quite believe my eyes. That they can justify their actions in the name of religion is quite incomprehensible to me, and I would dearly like to talk with them about it, if only to get it straight in my own mind. But none of these Jewish settlers have I ever found remotely approachable. Even on previous visits, whenever I did try to talk to them, I was never answered with anything other than a curse. Fortunately, there were Jews willing to make up for this reticence. After my visit to Gaza it became imperative for me to try to meet Jews who opposed what was happening in Israel.

Israel Shahak was one. I had only just been introduced to his book, *Jewish History, Jewish Religion*, and had stayed up late for several nights excited, challenged and disturbed by it in turn. I could quite see the book would not make Shahak popular with the Israeli establishment, since it declares openly that Israel as a Jewish state constitutes a danger not only to itself and its inhabitants, but to all Jews, and to all other peoples and states in the Middle East and beyond.

The book begins with an incident in 1965 when Shahak had witnessed an ultra-Orthodox Jew refusing to allow his phone to be used on the Sabbath in order to summon an ambulance for a non-Jew who had just suffered a heart attack outside his home. Shahak pursued this incident with the Rabbinical Court of Jerusalem who gave as their opinion that the Jew in question had behaved not only correctly, but indeed piously, in refusing to break the Sabbath to help a Gentile. They backed up their opinion with references to passages in the Talmudic laws, and in particular to one written in this century.

With great clarity Shahak's book goes on to explore the extent to which the secular state of Israel has been shaped by these religious ideas of an invidious and potentially lethal nature. While Muslim fundamentalism is execrated in the West, Shahak claims Jewish fundamentalism goes largely unremarked, although Israel pursues policies which are as racist, totalitarian and xenophobic as the worst excesses of anti-Semitism, all of which can be seen clearly in Jewish attitudes to the non-Jewish people of Israel and the Middle East.

A life-long human rights activist, Shahak's credentials make him a difficult man for Israel to dismiss out of hand. Born in Warsaw in 1933, he spent his childhood in Belsen concentration camp before coming to Israel as a boy of twelve. He became a highly respected Professor of Organic Chemistry, but must always have had a parallel interest in religion in general and the Talmud and rabbinical law in particular because his sheer breadth of knowledge in those subjects is awe-inspiring.

The Jewish writer, Gore Vidal, writing the foreword to Shahak's book claims him to be the latest of the great prophets. If he is so, then it is Jeremiah he most resembles; Jeremiah bravely preaching his doom-laden message to a Jerusalem threatened with imminent destruction by the Babylonians. With Nebuchadnezzar virtually at the gates of the city, Jeremiah was reckoned a dangerous fifth columnist sapping the will of the people, and was cast into a cistern. But the King had him pulled out secretly at night to ask him, 'Is there any word from the Lord?' There was, but only more of the same, and Jeremiah was cast back into the cistern. Two and a half thousand years later Shahak, who is guilty of spreading an equally seditious and uncompromising message is still free to publish his views, which gives me some hope for the future of Israel.

I would have appreciated more time to study Shahak's writings before I met him. As it was, I was hard pressed to ask the right questions in the generous half-hour he spared me from his work. Like many Christians, because our religion embraces so much of Jewish sacred literature, particularly the classical prophets, I had always assumed the two religions to have a great deal of common ground. Shahak's book had shaken me out of this false and cosy attitude, and left me adrift as to what, if anything, the two faiths did share. Never before had Christianity appeared so clearly as the great schism of the Jewish faith, though this theme had not at all been part of Shahak's book.

On the subject of spirituality we got nowhere. Shahak took the stand of 'religion being its own benefit, and something that cannot be allowed to corrupt society.' Ideologies were much the same. 'We are being ruled by ideologies and it does not work; ideals yes; ideology no.' Society was what mattered and must always come first. Justice also mattered, but it could only be expressed in secular terms in these times, and secular justice breaks down. You had to be content with little victories. He illustrated this with a story of Christians being taken around St Sophia in Istanbul by a Turk who told them it was forbidden for people to pray there. 'So one of them asks, does the ban include meditation? and the Turk says "No, that is allowed." You see? Small victory.' It was the way to look at early democracies also; they had slaves and were therefore flawed, but there was also much that was good in them.

To have the opportunity to pursue even a few thoughts with a man of such impressive intellect was something of an exercise in survival, though there was a great exhilaration in it too. I could feel my brain pushing out into unaccustomed ground. But over and above the sheer enjoyment of heady ideas, I felt an admiration for Shahak as a man. A person for whom truth is the ultimate and only goal can seem rather cold and academic, which was not at all the case with Israel Shahak, probably because of his insistence on the importance of the community.

He has to pay a heavy price for the stand he has taken against the politics of the country to which he is deeply committed. A small man, he appears older than his sixty years and deeply scarred by his experiences, but nonetheless he does not appear in the least defeated, and his wide involvement with life is wonderfully refreshing after the profound insularity of the average Israeli I met.

Another Jerusalem Israeli who was proudly Jewish but totally opposed to her country's injustices was the advocate Leah Tsemel. She was so overworked with her entirely Palestinian clientele that she suggested I accompany her on her rounds and we talked in her car as we shuttled to and fro between the military court at Ramallah and the civilian court in Jerusalem. I followed her well-groomed, rather heavy figure through both these courts, talking with her in her car, in the pauses between swallowing lunch as we drove. Her attendance at the military court was simply a request for an adjournment on a case, so we were quickly in and out. All I remember of it is the squalor of the shed-like building and the arrogance of the young army personnel presiding over the court, lounging about in sloppy army fatigues and chewing gum.

The Jerusalem court was housed in the old Russian Pilgrim Compound a little way up the Jaffa Road. Convenient if incongruous, with all the different buildings for torture, for questioning and the dispensation of justice, all kept decently separate. As I had already been told, compartmentalizing Israeli life makes it easier for the average Israeli to remain in ignorance of many of the abuses. Torturers and questioners, for example, are never the same people, and operate in different areas.

Leah was there on a sort of habeas corpus plea. Her client had been taken for questioning two weeks previously and apparently the only way a lawyer can get to see her client during the long initial questioning period is to apply for his release. I don't think she expected any favourable outcome. She thought it a good idea to get the man produced, and for the magistrate to see what shape he was in. Possibly it might also help prevent the automatic extension of the questioning period. The charge against the man was the usual one of being suspected of involvement in terrorist activity.

When we arrived at the court the prisoner's sister, brother and a friend were already there. The corridor of the former pilgrim hostel was the waiting area, with the refectory and common rooms serving as courts. The magistrate was already inside but no one had sent for the prisoner. Leah herself shouted at a warder to go and bring him. While we all sat and waited, quite suddenly the prisoner was being pushed down the corridor towards us. His hands were handcuffed behind his back and he appeared dazed and unfocused and very pale. His family rushed forward and tried to enter the courtroom with him, but they were stopped at the door and only Leah herself managed to squeeze inside.

While we waited the brother talked about the first time he was arrested. He had been tortured for the usual eighteen days, the guards being careful to leave no mark. 'So on the day we were going before the magistrate,' he said, 'another boy and I smashed our faces against the bars to make them bleed, so that the magistrate would see something.' I asked what happened. 'Nothing,' he said, 'The magistrate didn't even notice our faces but the guard did, he said: "Good, now we can do what we like with you." '

Leah came out and said she had left the court so that the magistrate could talk to her client as he was not allowed to say anything while she was there. Being kept strictly incommunicado was an important part of the eighteen day process; often families have no idea where their sons are during this period. When I met other Jewish activists who helped Palestinians I discovered that the entire work of one bureau was to keep track of arrests so that families could at least know where their sons, fathers or husbands had been taken.

The young prisoner made one more appearance as he was being hustled away, and, brief though it was, I can still remember that white vulnerable face. His family shouted messages of encouragement after him as he disappeared, standing there stiff with an anger and frustration you could almost touch. How does one begin to cope with the thought of a brother being handed back to the torturers?

Leah felt she could now spare an hour for my questions and we sat over coffee in a small street where quasi-artists' ateliers rub shoulders with boutiques and coffee shops. It was not really quite warm enough to sit outside, but after the sad dusty corridors we felt more comfortable in the open air.

It was the war of 1967 that first made her aware of the injustice of Israel's position, said Leah. She had been born in Haifa and didn't even know there were Arabs until then – having spent time in Israel myself, I can quite understand this – in Israel proper, as opposed to the occupied West Bank and Gaza, you hardly ever see an Arab. A few come in on a daily basis to work, returning to the territories by nightfall, and the few who are there permanently are Israeli Arabs who have chosen to become as much a part of Israel as they are allowed to be, serving in the army and so forth.

Leah was at university studying law when the realization of Israel as an aggressor first hit her with a startling force. The knowledge that Israel was actually creating refugees was almost unbearable to someone brought up in the belief of being a citizen of a virtuous country, a country that only defended itself, never attacked. For Leah, that was the beginning of a deep resentment which continued to be fuelled by the occupation and by the war of attrition in Lebanon.

Her political life began there and then at university with a small group of like-minded students. The schools were changing their curriculum at the time in order to cover recent events in a way that glorified the occupation and Leah and the other students tried to combat that by telling schoolchildren what really happened.

She married a like-minded activist who spent so much time in prison that she was the only bread winner of a family that soon included two children. Her son had found his parents' political activity particularly hard, and refused to be seen outside the house with them for fear of what his school friends would say. But after 1982 the former hatred of the Israeli public for 'anti-state activity' turned into a sort of adulation, and Leah's daughter, who was younger, was proud of her parents. Being able to say my father or my mother is in prison for anti-state activity apparently now carries a certain cachet.

I could imagine Leah Tsemel in no other field than law, nor of choosing to champion any but the afflicted and the down-trodden. Like Israel Shahak, her strength appeared to me to stem directly from a strong sense of her Jewishness, a Jewish-ness which confers not an innate and natural superiority, but rather demands standards and duties. With both of them I felt it was their passion for justice – which meant so much more than a mere dispensation of an equable law – that underpinned their very existence. Justice of this sort was a necessity of life like breathing; a self-evident truth. It felt very good in Israel's current climate to be reminded that the moral genius of the Old Testament prophets was by no means a dead notion of a forgotten past.

Linda Bayer was another Jewish advocate I met in Jerusalem, who was working on behalf of the Palestinians in the tricky field of land problems. Her horror stories of land confiscations and of Palestinian children coming back from school to find their house bulldozed by the army, on one spurious legal pretext or another, had all the pathos of Naboth's vineyard, and would need a book of their own to do them justice. But Linda had another role. She had recently converted to Roman Catholicism and was still in that giddy state of euphoria that often character-izes the new proselyte, and causes a certain amount of alarm to friends, new and old.

I warmed to her whole-heartedly only when I heard her address a gathering of three hundred American Methodist tourists gathered in a horrid pink room in an enormous hotel in West Jerusalem.

'I am a real Yidisha Grandmother and a Christian,' she began, and went on to give a picture of what life is like in Israel today which would have made Cecil B. de Mille hire her on the spot as the ideal script writer for a masterly simplification of difficult scenarios. Methodists flocked about her in droves after-wards to commiserate with her on the difficulties her conver-sion must have caused her.

I was convinced that Linda and other Jews like her who ran

relief agencies for the benefit of Palestinians, had the good of those they were helping at heart. But even added all together it seemed little more than window dressing. The exceptions like Leah Tsemel and Israel Shahak who paid a price, and often a heavy one, for their stand were few in number. Many of the agencies were well funded, and offered their employees a very comfortable lifestyle. There were a couple of magazines which published hard facts about the political situation, and whose Jewish editors had served periods in jail for subversive activity, but they were aimed at a particular and narrow fringe and did little to raise the general level of awareness. There were many Israelis who refused to do military service in the Occupied Territories, and while this was encouraging it was not a direct involvement in the Palestinian problem.

The only grass-roots Jewish movement, Peace Now, which might once have been a potent force, seemed to me to have become a very mild middle-class affair that actually provided Israel with a semblance of democratic freedom. Even the *Jerusalem Post*, an English language newspaper that had once had a refreshingly unbiased style of reporting appeared to have had its teeth pulled.

The attitude of the average Israeli seemed to me to be summed up succinctly and depressingly by a woman with whom I talked while we were both waiting for a bus in West Jerusalem. 'Look,' she said, 'It's very simple. This is our country. We have nowhere else to go. Palestinians have more than twenty other Arab countries to choose from. If they don't like it here they should go.'

CHAPTER FIFTEEN

Christians in Action

The Armenian Cathedral Church of St James is quite unlike any other church in Jerusalem in its atmosphere of mystery and sumptuous wealth. Accumulated treasures of diverse periods and styles adorn every wall and pillar; huge candelabras and strings of coloured lamps fill the vaulted spaces between the high-domed roof and the towering gilded reredos; altars dripping gold, icons, thrones and rich hangings make of it something of an Aladdin's cave, but one that is both holy and transcendent. Echoes of Byzantium, of Persia and of the Armenians' own ancient lands that once extended over the vast area between the Caspian and the Mediterranean Seas all find their place here. It is a lovely church at all times, but on a winter's evening when the innumerable lamps prick the vaulted darkness like frosted stars and the great towering altar is ablaze with candles striking fire from the golden vessels, the monstrances and the icons, it is superb.

It was one of the earliest of the Christian churches in Jerusalem though the present structure is largely Crusader-built, except for the beautiful central cupola which is pure Armenian. Armenians and Crusaders were natural allies and frequently intermarried, several Armenian women becoming Queens of Jerusalem. St James's Cathedral naturally benefited from these royal connections, but it had great claims to fame in its own right as the possessor of important relics.

Relics were the passion of medieval Christianity, prized above the most precious of jewels. The more venerated the saint, the more priceless his mortal remains. A church that could acquire even a few bones of a major saint soon found tremendous wealth accruing to it from the floods of rich pilgrims seeking heavenly merit or earthly healing through worship at these sanctified places. The gifts they brought to the shrine were intended to be worthy of the favours they sought.

St James's Cathedral was one such major shrine. Not only was it built upon the site of the beheading of the Apostle James, brother of John, who together with Peter had been present at all the principal events in the life of Christ, more importantly, the church also possessed that severed head. That both the head and body of St James were also claimed to rest in the Spanish Cathedral of Santiago de Compostela seemed not to matter overmuch to the medieval mind; it was not unusual for the same saint to be venerated in several different locations. As an added attraction St James's Cathedral also possessed the hand of the martyred St Stephen. Small wonder then that it should be so exceptionally filled with objects of wealth and beauty.

To be within St James's at all always seems a special privilege, since it is not the easiest of churches to visit. Unless one wishes to attend the daily service, it is necessary to telephone to ask for an appointment to view. This undoubtedly helps to preserve its atmosphere; and since the guardians of St James's make no efforts to attract tourists it can more easily insist upon its own standards of conduct. No clicking cameras or whirling camcorders are ever allowed to disturb the peace and sanctity, and even leaning against the wrong part of a wall in the vestibule can mean a gowned attendant coming to tell you gently but firmly that this is not allowed, as the spot is sacred to someone's memory.

Another treasure of the Armenian convent is the library of precious illuminated gospels and manuscripts. Many of these came from the villages of Eastern Turkey during the decades of the massacres. When the Turkish order came for Armenians to evacuate their houses and join the dreaded death marches, their priest would first toll the church bell to call all the people together (by this time it was only the women and children who were left, most of the men were already slaughtered). All newly-born infants would be hurriedly baptized, and the precious handwritten copy of the gospels would be given to the women, often cut into two or three pieces to make their concealment easier. That in spite of the inconceivable horror of those marches and the appalling number of deaths that littered the route, so many manuscripts, or portions of them eventually found their way to the library at Jerusalem says a great deal about the piety of the people. Together with the long history of the Armenians in the Holy Land it must also add considerably to the very special atmosphere of St James's.

A week of prayer for Christian Unity provided the rare opportunity of attending an ecumenical service in this lovely stronghold of the monophysite faith. As the worshippers gathered, each with a slim brown taper to illuminate their service sheet, Armenian bishops, faintly sinister in their tall, pointed black hoods and fluttering robes, drifted silently over the priceless Eastern carpets. Beneath the hanging skeins of coloured glass lamps, solid young seminarians in flowered cassocks sang a deep-throated Russian-style chant, while behind them the altar flared in a blaze of gold like a reproduction of Rembrandt's *Belshazzar's Feast*.

A night or two before this I had given my lecture in the Armenian Seminary, with the Patriarch in his rich robes seated among his bishops on a throne-like chair in the centre of the front row, eyeball to eyeball. It was my first experience of prefacing a talk with 'Your Beatitude, your Graces, Reverend Fathers . . .' but any sense of intimidation I might have felt soon wore off because of the rapt attention in the room – attention attributable to the subject rather than the skill of the speaker. As I retraced the route of my journey around Ararat and through their hereditary lands – which are also the seminal lands of the Old Testament, the lands of Noah and the Flood – I could see the audience savouring each and every place-name, rolling them around, tasting them on the tongue.

Only the very oldest of my audience could have the faintest memory of the places and landscapes I described; none had been able to go back to visit. But clearly they had never for a moment forgotten their roots. Their children had been reared on the history of their parents' terrible exodus and their own lost inheritance. Their delight in hearing from an outsider a first hand account of what were now their almost mystical 'Fields of

162

Elysium' was palpable. After the lecture I was detained for hours by young seminarians who wanted to put questions to me through an interpreter. These were nearly all detailed inquiries about specific places, tiny villages for the most part, whose names had been burned into their folk-memory. But there were also questions about the nature of Turkish people that revealed a desire to understand how the terrible events could have happened.

I thought of it now while the Armenian clergy and seminarians were setting this scene of solemn magnificence, and the rest of us – Lutherans, Latins, Greeks, Copts, Ethiopians, Jacobites, Anglicans, Maronites, Georgians, Russians, Syrians – representatives of all the many strands of the Christian Church whose adherents have worshipped in Jerusalem for centuries, crowded the shadowed spaces between the pillars. In these days of minimal church attendance, the sheer weight of our number was awe-inspiring. This and the wide diversity of worship that somehow could achieve a unity of the spirit was what made Jerusalem so special. Like the Armenians, we were all in a sense 'singing the Lord's song in a strange land', even those whose families went back to the first Pentecost and the times of Christ. But for all of us there, this was the seminal city of our faith, intended as a mirror of the true and the perfect, the Heavenly Jerusalem. A paradox of a city – a City of Strife, a City of Peace.

Within the magnificence of the setting and the ancient form of the liturgy that gave shape and rhythm to our worship, it was essentially a simple and moving service, and many of the prayers were in English (the new lingua franca that has replaced the Greek of Christ's day). As we held our brown, flickering tapers over our service sheets, members of each community, clergy and laity, took their turn in leading the prayers. People spoke with feeling and simplicity, so that the present troubles and the need for divine help with them had never seemed so real. The sense of unity even among outsiders like myself grew and spread through the church like a tangible increase in warmth and strength.

No concessions are made to human frailty in St James's, no 'women and children to the wall' here, for unlike other Eastern churches there are no seats to go to. For this service the Latin and the Greek Orthodox nuns had come sensibly prepared with folding stools, and were generous in sharing them with the older laity; a ten minute respite makes all the difference in a two hour service.

Many of the faces framed in their soft halo of candlelight I knew, and during the long Armenian passages and the beautiful chants I thought about conversations I'd had with them. There was old Dr Zihad, whose beautiful apartment in the Christian Quarter was in a key position to witness all the various take-overs of Jerusalem that had occurred in his long life. His family had for centuries been members of the Greek Orthodox Church. They were noted gold and silversmiths, though Dr Zihad himself was a dentist, trained in Beirut and long since retired.

He had been a young man between the wars, during the period of the British Mandate, and the expanding Jerusalem he had known in his youth now seemed a world away. 'The Old City was only for school and church,' he told me. 'You behaved in a special way there. All our entertainment and pleasure was outside the walls in East and West Jerusalem.' He remembers the shops and booths clinging, medieval style, to Jerusalem's walls between Jaffa and New Gate, and the rich suburbs growing up beyond them, with cinemas and shopping centres and other trappings of the rapidly changing twenties and thir-ties that made life so exciting for the young.

His family had built a big new house in the suburbs, which like most Palestinian houses, was commandeered by the Israelis in 1948. 'My family became refugees sheltered by the Greek Orthodox Convent, until I came back from studying in Beirut and we managed to buy this house. Now only I am left.'

'Jerusalem,' he told me once, 'is not a city. I am Jerusalem. It is like a marriage, part of me, my own self. I feel at one with these stones.' He cannot accept that Jerusalem is now in Israeli hands. 'Even under the Turks, life was better. As long as you paid your taxes you were left in peace. We never believed the Jews could take the Old City, even under Jordan we never

believed that. When I was a boy we went around all together –
Greeks, Arabs, Jews – the hatred was not like it is now, only
small. Some Jewish friends used to talk about their "programme". They had an obsession with Jerusalem, they swore
they would have it one day even if it meant the blood comes up
to here,' and he indicated a height somewhere around eye-level.
'We didn't take much notice. But now they do have it and they
want us all out; already they are pulling down so many fine
buildings; they want to impose the twentieth century on a
beautiful medieval town. They are spoiling Jerusalem. It is very
hard, for most of them are not religious.'

Among the Latins I could see Mr Freha, a sturdier figure
than frail Dr Zihad. He was an old friend of George's, sharing
his passion for nineteenth-century Holy Land history. Mr
Freha's wife was very active in Catholic relief work in the community and he himself ran a small marketing business from
Salah ed Din Street, just outside Damascus Gate. Whenever I
passed his office I was invited in to drink coffee, and I always
welcomed the chance to hear his unassuming but pithy reflec-
tions. It was Mr Freha who years before had first drawn my
attention to the diverse mixture of bloods that have homed in
on Jerusalem and mingled with the native stock, creating this
great diversity of worship, that so many people think a scandal.
'What does it matter?' he would ask with relish. 'There is one
God, worship him how you will. The same with Jerusalem –
many voices but a universe of prayer. I have nothing against
Muslims or Jews: for them too there is but one God. But Israeli
is not Jew. It is not co-existence here now, but a rubbing out.'

Mary Egavian, an Armenian woman married to a Palestinian
Roman Catholic was leading the prayers for her community.
She was one of the most impressive and tireless workers for
peace I knew in Jerusalem, and she saw her role very clearly as a
bridge between Muslims and Jews. 'We Christians are unique
among the religions of Jerusalem. We have to forgive, we don't
have a choice about that, as do the Jews and Muslims.' She also
explained the special opportunity presented to Christian
women in the present troubles. When Christian Palestinian men
lose their jobs, or are imprisoned, or in other ways prevented

from being able to provide for their families, women naturally take on the role of bread winner. For Muslim families it is far more difficult because traditionally it is not considered respectable for women to work outside the home. Christian women have helped in this by encouraging Muslim women in the skills that can be pursued at home, and by marketing whatever the women produce – often quite stunning embroideries and clothing. 'Throughout the *intifada* the supportive role in all aspects of our life – human rights, education, medicine, economic relief – has been undertaken by women,' said Mary. 'We make no distinction between Muslim and Christian, all need our help. This has given a validity to the Christian presence here and to our role as witnesses speaking out against the injustices.'

So many strong women have emerged to meet the challenge of living in Jerusalem in these times. Another of them present at this service was Claudette, a woman small in stature but with the heart of a lion and nerves of steel. She also comes of a wealthy Palestinian family, and as so many Palestinians like her must do, she has daily to pass her family's confiscated house, an elegant mansion just outside Jerusalem's walls. This house is now used by the Israelis for public functions and ironically, Claudette was once invited to give a talk there on her particular aspect of social work. The audience of course had no idea of her connection with the house and were, she said, as surprised as she was herself when, instead of the usual opening remarks, she found herself saying: 'You are all welcome in my family home, and I am so pleased to see you have not removed my mother's piano from the place where she left it.'

After she had delivered herself of this unconscious weight, she said she was able to proceed with the talk as though nothing untoward had happened. 'They probably thought I was mad,' she joked. Claudette joked a great deal, and I found that this tendency to make light of suffering, to use humour as a safety-valve, was more typical of the women of Jerusalem than the men. No matter how serious the subject discussed, there was nearly always room for laughter, and I was never made more aware of its healing quality.

Claudette's role had not always been so peaceful, I gathered, especially not during the *intifada*, when she risked arrest on many occasions. But activities like breaking curfews, getting involved in banned political activity and the like she now considers a waste of her valuable time. Like Mary she feels her life can only be justified by service to others, and from the accounts I heard from others about the extent of her involvement in various relief projects, she does the work of three normal women. Claudette herself sees her life as coming full circle. She can remember her father trying to teach her that it was conscience that ultimately really mattered. 'Now,' says Claudette, 'I know what he meant. I too sleep well at nights, and I feel that I am ready at any time to meet my maker. Nobody can take that away.'

One face I missed at this service of Christian Unity was Mrs Jean Zaru, a Quaker woman I had gone to see in Ramallah, a former stronghold of Christianity. Although just fifteen minutes drive from the Old City, Ramallah being part of the West Bank is more or less permanently cut off from Jerusalem. Neither Christians nor Muslims can pursue careers in Jerusalem, nor can they worship in what for both is the central shrine of their faith, just as two thousand years before the Romans placed the same embargo on the Jews.

Mrs Zaru comes of an old and highly-respected Palestinian Christian family, the sort that is usually the backbone of any community. She had been educated in the prestigious Society of Friends Girls School in Ramallah, and is internationally known for her work for Christian unity, a role that requires frequent attendance at various international councils.

The process that Israeli bureaucracy requires Palestinians to go through in order to make any international journey would defeat most lesser women, particularly a grandmother of the age of Mrs Zaru. Days and days of exhaustive red tape must be gone through, coupled with a considerable outlay of cash, and all resulting in a permit valid for just one journey. To have to go through that several times a year hardly bears thinking about.

Jean had passed quickly over the familiar tale of the erosion of the family's modest wealth and seizure of property, the years that have to elapse before a sale of property goes through and the impossibility of getting at money in foreign banks. Far worse are the personal tragedies, like the brother studying abroad at the time of the Six Day War when Israel decided any Palestinian absent from the country for any reason whatsoever would not be allowed back in. Many young students, desperate and embittered by their enforced exile, cut off permanently from their families found a natural answer in joining Arafat or some other freedom-fighting/terrorist organization. Many became the 'disappeared of Lebanon' never to be heard of again.

Jean's ability to outline the structures that cause the daily pressures under which Palestinians live was particularly helpful to me. She described them as three-fold. The political problem is quite simply the eroding of all the rights and identity of Palestinian people. Palestinian territory, defined by the UN in 1948 and now known as the Occupied Territories, consists of only 22 per cent of Palestine, and since the occupation, 50 per cent of that has been taken by the Israelis to build settlements.

The social problems result in daily living conditions that are continuously deteriorating. Boxed up in these shrunken territories, paying high taxes to Israel who puts no money into supporting any kind of social infrastructure – there are, for example, no traffic lights in most of the towns of the Occupied Territories, no waste disposal, no road repairs, virtually no services of any kind – everything slowly erodes and order gives way to chaos.

Christian Zionism as the third aspect of the problem I had at first questioned, having thought the movement too idiotic to pose a threat. But Jean Zaru was adamant about the extent of the damage created through the 'International Christian Embassy' that every night broadcasts its distorting Zionist messages, setting the State of Israel upon a pedestal, and advancing the idea of Christians doing God's work in placing 'God's Special and Chosen People' in the position intended for them.

This distortion of Christianity, Jean declares, has led to its erosion among the Christian communities as well as perverting its image among their Muslim neighbours. By so doing it saps the very bedrock of Palestinian society, and seen like that it is not difficult to appreciate how truly sinister it is.

Someone whose writings also endorsed this view of the extremely damaging role of Christian Zionism is Canon Na'im Ateek, who was representing the Anglican community of St George's Cathedral in East Jerusalem.

As a boy of ten, the son of a Christian minister in Beit Shean, Na'im Ateek together with his family had been expelled from his house at gunpoint, his father's pleas to be allowed to remain and minister to his flock falling upon deaf ears. He had therefore been forced at an early age to wrestle with the nitty-gritty of Christian ethics. Of all the voices unequivocally spelling out the Christian's role in present day Jerusalem, I found Canon Ateek's one of the most impressive.

An unexpected pleasure of this particular visit had been hearing some of his series of sermons on the theme of Christianity and violence. A gifted thinker and writer, he is also that modern rarity, an inspired and fearless preacher. Actually he had to deliver two sermons on each occasion I heard him, one to his own flock of Arabic speakers, followed by a translation in English for the huge gatherings of foreign Christians who packed every foot of space in the cathedral, even to sitting on the steps of the font and the organ. Ten years of study in America had made the Canon equally skilled in both tongues.

Being on the tourist circuit was, he told me, a two-edged honour since, first and foremost, he felt his duty was to his own beleaguered flock, and he did not want them taking second place to the infinitely larger foreign congregation.

The foundation of the Canon's sermons was the same idea or belief that had struck me so powerfully, though rather more intuitively, on my first days in Jerusalem. Namely that the Holy Land today under the Israeli occupation almost exactly mirrors first century Palestine under the Roman occupation, and that the unjust and exploitative conditions under which Christ himself lived and which he had spoken out against so forcibly, are almost exactly duplicated by what his followers suffer in present day Israel. All of which of course gives a special poignancy, but also a pressing reality to the teaching of Christ.

Drawing on gospel accounts to point out parallel after parallel, Canon Ateek exposed the whole gamut of abuses that had afflicted the population then as now, from the use of soldiers for the gathering of punitive taxes, shameless exploitation and confiscation of land and property, the bending of laws, imprisonment and harshness of all kinds – in short all the hundred and one ills that lead to widespread poverty, and to crime and lawlessness to the point where bands of thieves rove the streets – a phenomenon that increasingly makes today's news.

He drew equally on the Old Testament which, as he pointed out, is filled with God's call for justice and righteousness. Through the prophets also comes the disproving of the notion of a 'chosen people' to be replaced by the idea of a universal and inclusive God who has no favourite people or nation, an idea which grew and found its culmination in the gospels.

It is not possible in a few paragraphs to do justice to the scope and power of Canon Ateek's scholarly arguments, but one parallel I remember particularly was his brave debunking of the Zealots, the folk-heroes of their day. Soon after the death of Christ, the Zealots rebelled against Roman misrule. Incredibly successful though the rebellion proved in the short term, it was really a worthless exercise, for it led to the destruction of Jerusalem and to the final and total ruin of the Jewish nation. 'If in place of Zealots you substitute Hamas,' suggested the Canon, 'and instead of seeing them as heroes, you put them in the same category as a present-day thug or a terrorist, then you have a quite different picture. Religious extremism in history (and in the present day) is nearly always closely coupled with extreme violence.

'For Christians,' he summed up, 'all violence is unequivocally evil, and the gospels oppose it absolutely, substituting in its place love, truth and justice. As Christians we have no choice but to stand totally opposed to violence, and to name it for what it is – evil. We have to purge violence from ourselves at an individual level, while at the same time never ceasing to speak out fearlessly against injustice.'

I don't know if I would have found Canon Ateek so inspiring had I not spent enough time among Holy Land Christians to realize the life and death immediacy of his message. In the situation prevailing there today Christians clearly have no choice, no time to prevaricate; you are either swallowed up in the violence, the hatred and the bitterness, or you fight it with the only tools powerful enough to prevail, the tools of love, truth and forgiveness.

Back home among the seemingly less urgent concerns of falling church attendance, the erosion of language and beauty in our worship, the decline of spirituality and our gross materialism, I feel we are playing at religion. Then I am homesick for Jerusalem and its clearer canvas. And yet I also know the message is the same and the immediacy just as great, even if it is easier to ignore than in Jerusalem.

Faces lit by tapers in the setting of a lovely church, I see them when I think of Jerusalem, but the picture has widened now to include other faces, many of whom would certainly not claim to be followers of Christ. Some indeed are Muslims, some Jews, some follow no creed at all, and some are simply faces glimpsed across an ill-equipped clinic or a makeshift classroom. Together they make up an 'army of the faithful'. What all have in common is that at an individual level they have made the decision not to go with the tide, not to be conquered by violence and hatred. They fight evil with love and with service to their fellow men, as St Stephen, the proto-martyr, did before them. And as with Stephen, whose 'face was like an angel' they too have something quite recognizably different about them.

CHAPTER SIXTEEN

Friday in Jerusalem

Friday in Jerusalem is the first of the week's three holy days, the day especially sacred to Muslims. From an early hour, worshippers flood in through Damascus Gate as they have done for centuries to pray in the mosques on the Temple Mount. For the Israeli authorities, obsessed by security, Friday is a fraught day and doubly so during this season of Ramadan when numbers are greater than usual, and violence and acts of terrorism thought to be more likely.

But dense though the crowds are, the numbers of worshippers have been much reduced over recent years. The iron cordon around the Occupied Territories means that thousands of Palestinian Muslims who would make it their duty to worship in Jerusalem during Ramadan are prevented from doing so, as is the case for their Christian brothers at Easter and other religious festivals. Every incident, whether caused by Arab or by Jewish extremists, is an excuse to close the territories. Shopkeepers in the bazaars who rely on the increased trade of Ramadan and the major festivals grow ever poorer. Many of them also have their stores vandalized by the more violent Jewish settlers against whom they dare not retaliate for fear of savage reprisals. This and the taxes that bite ever deeper force more and more native Jerusalem families out of business and out of the city.

From early morning Israeli border guard soldiers have been assembling in the city in large numbers. They come by truckloads to a corner of the Wailing Wall piazza. On my way to early mass at Holy Sepulchre I see them being marched, clad in full riot gear and heavily armed, to strategic points along the streets of the Muslim Quarter. These soldiers are regular army troops, by reputation very tough and mostly Sephardic Jews from North Africa, their looks indistinguishable from Arabs. Only the whiter-skinned officers who march beside them appear to be of European Ashkenazim descent. The soldiers' uniforms and weapons and their air of detachment from their surroundings once again call up memories of Rome with its well-drilled legions of foreign mercenaries, tolerant of the barbarians they rule over so long as they give no trouble.

Muslim worshippers converging on the Noble Sanctuary are forced to witness the changing status of their Quarter of Jerusalem. Hebrew graffiti litter the walls of Muslim houses which the settlers hope to 'redeem', these include ancient Islamic public buildings of great beauty. Buildings already 'redeemed' are covered in chalked stars of David or draped in outsize blue and white Israeli flags. Worshippers must also run the gauntlet of spot checks, body searches, and the sniffer dogs. The touch of these dogs is particularly offensive to Muslims for it defiles their carefully prepared ritual purity, and after such contact they must repeat their ablutions.

The air of tension is increased by the Jewish settlers of Jerusalem, particularly those who have established their foothold in the Muslim Quarter. They maintain a high profile on Fridays, strutting around the approaches to the Noble Sanctuary like characters from a period drama. Their heavy black beards, black homburg hats that just fail to cover the entirety of the black skullcaps beneath, and black unbuttoned overcoats that allow a glimpse of fringed prayer shawls contrast with the business-like automatic weapons slung over well-padded shoulders.

The soldiers pay no attention to the bizarre figures of the settlers. The extreme right-wing element of Israel is not yet taken seriously, for the nation-shattering event of Prime Minister Rabin's assassination by a fellow Jew is still eight and a half months away. All intimations that such an unthinkable deed could be possible are, at this time, ignored. With hindsight it can be seen that there have been ample warnings of the dangerous moral climate that has resulted from twenty-eight years of occupation. With hindsight the enemy within should have been recognized.

The massacre of Muslim men and boys at prayer in the mosque at Hebron could have been enough to alert the country to a situation that needed to be urgently addressed, especially so when the obscene act was greeted with such open joy by a very large section of the Israeli right. Instead the murder was played down and said to be the act of one isolated madman.

Palestinians convicted of an act of terrorism, even the minor one of lobbing a Molotov cocktail at an army truck are likely to have their house demolished as part of the punishment. The picture of families squatting beside the rubble of their bulldozed homes has become one of the most common symbols of Israeli occupation. The same treatment was demanded in respect of the family home of the perpetrator of the Hebron massacre, but the authorities argued that such a measure was unnecessary in this case, as the murderer, Goldstein, was not part of a general movement, so there was no need to make an example of him.

When, a year later, Goldstein's self-professed followers announced celebrations to mark the anniversary of his death, huge crowds of right-wing Israelis gathered to elevate the killer to a position of national hero and martyr. Their credo was the firm conviction that the whole land of Ancient Israel – the area of the Middle East held for just a few short decades by King David and his son Solomon – was Jewish land promised to them by God. Anyone who ceded a foot of it to anyone other than a Jew was a traitor, and anyone who helped rid the land of non-Jews was a hero. At which point a whole battery of alarms should have sounded throughout the state of Israel. But they did not. No one, it seems, except for a few modern prophets, like Israel Shahak, took any heed. For although most decent-minded Israelis condemned both the massacre and the celebrations, it was Jew against Arab; Jew against the traditional enemy. It was not yet the unthinkable, not Jew murdering Jew.

At the time of my visit evil was still something outside the State of Israel, something that concerned other races, not a part of the Jewish nation. There was as yet no acceptance of the possibility of an enemy within. It was to take the assassination of a

Jewish Head of State to do that – the murder of a Jew working to establish peace gunned down by a fellow Jew who claimed he was carrying out the will of God.

This particular morning, my last Friday in Jerusalem and some nine months before the assassination of Rabin I had an appointment with Hanan Ashrawi. She was someone I particularly wanted to meet for I had long admired her. Of all the people who in recent years had represented Palestine in the peace talks organized by America, it was Hanan Ashrawi who had done most to present a clear and reasonable picture of the Palestinian position to the world at large. An impressive and scholarly speaker she was clearly at home in the world of international diplomacy in a way that had never been possible for Arafat.

For decades the West's image of the Palestinian struggle had been dominated by the small, indomitable, rather scruffy figure in a traditional Arab headdress, and to a world implacably opposed to international terrorism, Arafat had enjoyed little appeal. I too had found it increasingly difficult to understand why he was held in such high esteem by the Palestinians. It certainly did not square with what I knew of their ideals or with their level of sophistication. But as any criticism of Arafat was sure to meet with an untypical reserve and hostility, I ceased trying to solve the apparent contradiction.

But now that Arafat the freedom fighter, exiled for so long in Tunisia, was at last the official leader of his people and in the process of metamorphosis from hated terrorist to respectable politician – a change, incidentally, long since effected by most of the present Israeli leadership – I could put the question that had puzzled me for so long. 'Why Arafat?' no longer provoked hostility, for many Palestinians were already asking themselves the same question, and if peace ever succeeded in becoming a reality and elections could at last take place, it would become the major issue.

I had already put the question to many Palestinians, including several who had been present at the preliminary peace talks in America. The simple and invariable answer to 'Why Arafat?' was 'Because there was no one else.' It was an answer that finally brought home to me the enormity of the predicament Palestinians had faced under Israeli occupation in a way that no litany of abuses and hardships could have done. For it revealed a frightening abyss of hopelessness which I, as a fully enfranchised citizen of a reasonably democratic country, could only imagine.

In the West we perhaps take our rights and freedoms too much for granted, forgetting the struggles – fights to the death sometimes – that have gone to establishing even our basic rights to parliamentary representation. For the last twenty-eight years, ever since the Israeli occupation of the remaining lands allotted to them by the United Nations, Palestinians' rights have been consistently eroded. At the same time Palestinians have been denied any political representation whatsoever. With no legal means of fighting back against the appropriation of their land and property, no means of fighting the endless injustices and the crippling punitive taxes, and with their plight more or less ignored by all international bodies, it was Arafat, and Arafat alone who offered them any kind of hope. It was Arafat who kept the Palestinian cause in the world's eye, and tirelessly proclaimed their right to exist. No matter how flawed his methods, he was their one bulwark against despair, the symbol of their nation. Now, as King Hussein had said, it remained to be seen whether the symbol could become a father to his people.

In this period of stalemate, a year after the declaration of peace, it was clear that Arafat no longer held his unassailable position with Palestinians. Probably no one could have done so.

To get to my appointment with Hanan Ashrawi in East Jerusalem I cycled around the outside of the walls to avoid the dense crowds at Damascus Gate. As soon as I had dropped down the hill from New Gate, however, I found the road cordoned off and was stopped at the barrier by a burly policeman wearing very dark sun-glasses. In a strong Brooklyn accent he demanded that I open up my handlebar bag. Reacting to his hectoring manner and his general swagger, I asked: 'Since when has Israel started to harass its foreign visitors?' 'See here lady,' he said, fixing me with a stare over the top of his impenetrable glasses and tapping his pistol holster significantly. 'The problem is we have to live here with savages who set off bombs.' 'What savages?' I asked, stung into a meaningless exchange. 'You are the only ones that I can see with weapons.' 'Come over here lady and I'll tell you about it,' he rejoined hotly. But I had had enough of confrontation for one day and declined, saying I had better things to do.

There was room enough to cycle on around his metal barrier, and he made no effort to stop me, nor had he actually bothered to look in my bag. Either he too was bored with meaningless confrontation or more likely he had decided I did not look like a likely 'savage with a bomb'.

On Hanan Ashrawi's door was a neat plate which read 'The Palestinian Independent Commission For Citizen's Rights'. When Arafat made his own secret backdoor peace with the Israelis in Oslo while his official peace delegation was still in America, arguing over the conditions he himself had demanded, the negotiators were naturally 'not amused'. Hanan Ashrawi had refused a position in Arafat's new government. Instead she had elected to head this watchdog commission. Her role as she sees it is trying to make sure that Palestine does not in its turn repeat the abuses of human rights that Israel has done in the Holy Land. 'A nation that has been abused is always in danger of abusing others in its turn,' Ashrawi explains, and indeed one can see examples of this all over the world, and nowhere more so than in this particular part of it. Hanan Ashrawi feels that it is a problem that must be addressed from the very outset. Already, she tells me, two prisoners have died under National Authority questioning.

I assume that her acceptance of this particular job means she has greater faith in the present peace process than have most of her former colleagues on the peace talks. But this is not at all the case. She shares in the general disillusionment. The only national leader to enjoy universal respect, she tells me, is Nelson Mandela; Arafat is about self-aggrandizement. The best thing to be said about the Oslo agreement, she continues is that it had gaps, but the subsequent agreement in Cairo has quashed any possibility of those gaps being filled in Palestine's favour. I suggest that there might be significant movements within Israel itself for a more just approach to the Palestinians, but she dismisses these as far too few to be effective.

Altogether Hanan Ashrawi left me with the impression that she sees Palestine still locked into a dark period of its history. The possibilities the *intifada* had given were now gone, and the inner strengths it had fostered would fade. An inspiringly clear and courageous thinker she certainly is, and someone whose abilities should be a great asset to her nation. But precisely because she is so impressive and level-headed, the fact that she seemed to hold out so little hope for an immediate or even a foreseeable solution to the problems of the Holy Land, left me feeling decidedly flattened.

Back in the Old City I took refuge, as I often did when depressed by the present, on the roof of Holy Sepulchre, in the peace and quiet of the old refectory of the Knights Templar. In those long-since ruined spaces where the little cells of the Ethiopian monks perch, transitory among the great weight of history, it is possible to be aware of a different scale of time and reality and to take comfort from it.

One of the elusive wary cats of the Quarter came to where I stood resting against a sunny wall. In a rare moment of trust for one of these persecuted creatures, it jumped up and rubbed itself against me, arching its back, offering itself to be stroked, and I was only too happy to oblige. A passing monk, taking in this picture of mutual comfort made a soft sound of approval and laid a hand lightly on my shoulder as he passed. For some reason I felt as though a weight had dropped off me.

Leaving the Ethiopians' roof by way of the Coptic Convent, I passed the entrance to the Empress Helena's cistern and realized that in all the times I had visited Jerusalem I had never once gone down to see this historical work. The Empress was said to have had it constructed in the fourth century AD to facilitate the enormous amounts of building work which her discoveries of the Holy Places had unleashed. Arriving there now at a time when it was open to visitors I descended the long flight of slippery rough-hewn steps and came to the huge underground pool cut in the rock and rendered impressively

Friday in Jerusalem

atmospheric by green lighting which was blinking off and on at the whim of an erratic electrical supply. As always I found it thrilling to see a work of antiquity on a grand scale that still serves its original function, but there was nothing more than that to hold me there and I turned to retrace my steps.

At that point however the light went out altogether, and while waiting for it to come on again I found myself deep in conversation with a young Jewish man who was also visiting the cistern. Perhaps the sudden plunge into darkness cut through the usual bland exchanges of strangers for almost immediately we were locked into politics. I found myself telling him how shocking I had found conditions in his country, especially in Gaza, while he told me about his military service there and how he had hated it. We might have been on line for a head-on confrontation, but in the darkness I had a sudden vision of him as a vulnerable youth frightened to death among the daunting alleyways I had visited in the camps of Gaza. I could imagine his flesh cringing in anticipation of a hail of cutting stones or petrol bombs which at any moment could come hurtling at him from a score of directions.

Perhaps my feeling of empathy communicated itself to him and made him receptive to the very different perceptions I had of his country. We continued our talk there by the handrail, with the light going off and on, revealing patches of the ancient chiselled surfaces and the dark, still water. I could see that Gaza would be a terrifying place in which to do one's military service, I said, but the worst aspect must be the corrupting influence of the experience. We talked about the bulldozing of houses, the harassment of civilians, the beatings and the policy of breaking the bones of children. I told him about the children I had seen who had been permanently maimed by Israeli soldiers, including the little paralysed 'martyr' shot while climbing up to fix a Palestinian flag to a roof.

'Yes,' he sighed, 'the army is corrupting, but Israel is not just the army.' 'But who in Israel,' I asked, 'does not serve in the army?' 'No one,' he agreed, 'but many now refuse to serve in the Occupied Territories.' I did not ask him if he himself had made such a decision, in case he had not. Suddenly I wanted to

179

get away before either of us might say something that would spoil the sympathy and accord we had built there in those green, echoing spaces of the cistern. I felt, I realized suddenly, as though I had been fraternizing with the enemy, and had found him to be just another human being locked in the same moral maze in which we all struggle. 'Look for small victories,' Israel Shahak had said; I felt that this was possibly one such.

The last of the day's engagements was the launch of a book about Christians in the Holy Land today. It was to be held in the ornate Sacré Cœur building just outside the walls, across the street from New Gate. I wanted to learn what I could of the church's own ideas about its future in Jerusalem, and since this was an occasion when several of the heavyweights of the various churches would be gathered, as well as those who had become my friends over the years, it would seem fruitful ground in which to feel the pulse of ecclesiastical opinion.

The current hot debate was the 'cemetery wars' and the continued pressure on Christian churches to provide burial space for the non-Jewish spouses of Jewish 'returnees', particularly those of the recent waves of Russian immigrants. I had not fully appreciated the taboos that surround Jewish burial and which extend to all Israeli citizens no matter whether professedly religious or not. Not only may a non-Jewish marriage partner not be buried alongside the spouse, they may not be interred at all in a Jewish burial ground. A Druse soldier serving in the Israeli army for instance may not be buried in the same plot as a Jewish soldier, even when the two fall together in the same battle. The lengths to which this separation is carried when trying to sort out the bits of body in a major explosion does not bear thinking about. Macabre though it might seem, it is nonetheless a very contentious issue. The whole subject is litigious, for often the burial space demanded from Palestinian Christians is for non-Jews brought into the country by Israel and settled on expropriated Palestinian land. With the increase in 'mixed' marriages it is a growing problem.

The issue I wanted to discuss, however, was the one I had heard mentioned wherever I went in Jerusalem, namely the status of the Holy City itself and the refusal of the Israeli

Government to give international guarantees concerning access to the Holy Sites and protection of Christians and their property. It took very little effort on my part to raise the subject, and many of those present were drawn into the resulting discussion, perhaps in spite of themselves, like a tongue returning to worry at a painful tooth. Skilled diplomats most of them, they were used to keeping a guard on what they said, but so angry had people become over what they saw as the Government's double dealing that emotions boiled over and caution was blown to the wind. 'To be a custodian of the holiest sites of Christendom can never have been more onerous a duty than it is today. If after two thousand years of Christian worship the last church is finally to close and the last congregation about to disappear how will one's stewardship be viewed?' asked one priest.

The nightmare scenario of Jerusalem's future painted by one bishop was of the Holy City as a mini-Harlem, a suburb lost in the huge amorphous mass of a Greater Jerusalem, itself ringed with barbed wire. There would be a token preservation of the sites for tourists, but the churches themselves would be empty shells.

Considering the marginalization of the Arab population and the rapid whittling away of the country's Christian congregations it was, as I now knew, a very real possibility that there would soon be no worshipping community in Jerusalem. And where there were no congregations what would happen to the Holy Places?

The idea ascribed to David Ben-Gurion, of having the walls of Jerusalem demolished so as to make the ancient city a part of West Jerusalem, was said to have changed to something more subtle, something that the world was less likely to notice and be up in arms over. The 'walled and gated city builded upon a hill' is disappearing quietly as the modern town creeps up upon it like a besieging army, filling in the spaces, raising the levels, so that eventually it will not matter if the walls do go, since they will no longer be seen until you are right upon them.

A new raised road for traffic is poised to pierce the ancient fabric near the Jaffa Gate. Even within the walls a policy of tasteless 'modernization' is changing the face of the medieval city.

But perhaps the greatest threat of all to the status of the Holy City is America's decision to move its embassy from Tel Aviv to Jerusalem. This is in defiance of other UN member states, all of whom have until now resisted Israel's efforts to establish Jerusalem as the official capital on the grounds that the Holy City itself, together with its northern and eastern environs, remains occupied territory.

Was there, I asked, no hope at all of a solution that would safeguard the interests of all concerned and preserve the city, which was arguably of greater significance to more people than any other place in history? What, for instance, of the original UN idea of making Jerusalem an international city?

That would never have worked, I was told, the idea was now as dead as was a return to the idea of a *corpus separatum* which once made a triangle of Christian land incorporating Bethlehem and the surrounding Christian villages. But there was one possible solution, an idea that had come from several sources, both Muslim and Christian. It was that Jerusalem should become a separate zone, rather like a national park where special laws apply. There would be free access for all worshippers of all faiths; autonomy for each holy shrine, and a restriction of sovereignty of power within. A similar arrangement to the one that already works well in Rome, both for the Vatican and the capital.

Such an arrangement would allow Israel to make Jerusalem its capital without infringing anyone's rights and without the necessity of continuing to occupy other people's land. Israelis would also have their rights in the Holy City like anyone else, and their parliament is already situated in undisputed West Jerusalem.

By the same token there would be nothing to stop the new state of Palestine having Jerusalem as her capital too. Both nations would begin and end outside the walls, each on its own land allotted to them by the UN in 1948. Nor need there be any wall to divide the two nations, for the Holy City would stand squarely between them, a city of peace open to all. Compared with the 'impregnable ghetto' mentality behind the present policies such a solution would at least have a working chance.

There was no one I spoke with among this gathering of people so long experienced in the problems of this part of the world who did not think that Israel's present policies would lead in the end to her own downfall, if for no other reason than because of the demographic inequalities. For, it appears to be an irrefutable argument that the more the Arabs are kept down and marginalized, the more they breed. At the present reckoning the Muslim birth rate is reckoned to be almost double that of the Jewish, which is still declining.

I would also say that there were few, if any, present among these Christians who felt anything but sorrow at the prospect of such an outcome. For insane though present Israeli policies seem, both dishonest and employing double standards, nonetheless Israel, both historically and in the present, holds a special place in the world's heart. It would indeed be a tragedy if once again, through inability to find a workable and lasting peace with her neighbours, she ceased to be.

As I walked back into the city through New Gate, the paved and cobbled ways of the Christian Quarter echoed emptily to my footsteps. Although not yet nine o'clock there was not a soul about for Jerusalem shuts down at nightfall as though it is already a half-dead city. Above the roofline of the stepped and twisting ways the sky was a midnight blue canopy filled with bright winter stars, each one rimmed with a frosty halo, as in a Samuel Palmer landscape. I made a detour down past the Greek Patriarchate to arrive at Holy Sepulchre by what I think of as the back way, passing the mosque of Omar and the row of little shops selling candles and incense and holy pictures.

Holy Sepulchre was locked as I knew it would be. But at night time the worn and broken stones of the courtyard flanked by the high walls and the battered Crusader entrance to the church offers something it lacks by day. Released from the milling crowds of tourists, the camcorders and the souvenir sellers, the centuries can seep out from the shadows. Many pilgrims have sat here on this low wall, seeing these same silhouettes of roofs and turrets, praying for the peace of Jerusalem, probing the seemingly insoluble dilemma. Something of their thoughts and prayers reaches across the great intervening spaces of time and death. Or so it seems to me. It does not make the pattern clearer, nor do the problems of the present grow any the less, but it makes for a sense of continuity that is all important.

As I made my way homeward through the Christian Quarter, I crossed the Muristan and saw by the rash of defiant Israeli flags draped across the upper floors of buildings that this site of the ancient hospital of the Knights of St John was also currently being 'redeemed'. Even climbing the narrow winding St Mark's Road, where Bishop Dionysus presides over his little Syriac Church rich in its treasures of an Upper Room and a painting of the Virgin Mary attributed to St Luke, I was aware of new Jewish houses and apartments pressing in, as they do in the Armenian Quarter. How long before the last of the Christian streets is 'redeemed', when the whole Quarter, together with the Muslim Quarter and the Armenian Quarter are all 'redeemed', swallowed up by Jewish fundamentalism?

Before reaching my spartan billet under the walls of St James's, I paused for one last look at this city spread out below me, wondering whether I would ever return. If I did what would I find? Would I even want to come here if it becomes just an amorphous suburb in a modern Middle Eastern city?

It would be easy to say that it is the idea of Jerusalem and what it represents that is important, and that the city itself is of lesser consequence. But I don't believe that. Jerusalem is so much more than an idea or a symbol. Christianity is rooted in history, as is Judaism and Islam, and as such Jerusalem is the tangible focus of God active in his Creation; God in our midst, the supreme place of pilgrimage.

We need Jerusalem. The very stones are important, the sites they solemnize even more so, and the continuity of the worshipping communities most of all. If the role of the earthly Jerusalem is to mirror the Heavenly Jerusalem, to be many voices 'creating a universe of prayer' as my friend in Salah ed Din Street had expressed it, then the mirror must be in place.

Jerusalem has been destroyed many times in the past. Phoenix-like it has always emerged from its ashes. Burnt down, destroyed, flattened, abandoned, even renamed it has always arisen again, which is no small indication of the importance it holds for a very great part of the world's people. What could we put in its place today? If this generation fails to protect Jerusalem, if we continue to allow the present erosion of its life and fabric, we and our children's children will be immeasurably the poorer.

CHAPTER SEVENTEEN

Water in a Dry Land

My journey to the Holy Land was at an end, a fact I viewed with mixed emotions. It had been a strange journey, very short in terms of miles pedalled, and with most of it spent in one small place, the walled city of Jerusalem. In terms of experience, however, it felt like one of the longest journeys I had ever made, as well as one of the most exhausting. Much as I had longed at times to be home again, away from the unbearable tensions of this divided land, now that departure was at hand I felt a great reluctance to leave. It was not simply the now familiar Holy Places and the rich diversity of worship I would miss. Far harder would be the turning of my back on the sense of purpose and commitment running like a strong thread through all the pain and hardships of life in the Holy Land. I felt as though I had seen Christianity working in its fullness for the very first time; seen as an everyday part of life 'the dying of the self to love'. Religion lived in this way is an exciting and compelling force, a far cry from the apathy and inertia that underlies so much of what passes for religion in much of the Western world today. It was this strong sense of mission that was hard to leave.

My simplest way home was to cycle north to Haifa, from where I could take a ship to Cyprus, docking in the port of Limassol which I had left just two months before, though it seemed more like years than months. I had to make sure I reached Haifa in good time as I had booked on the very last ship that would connect with my flight to England, and a speaking engagement that had been arranged for the day of my return. In spite of my precautions, however, the ship nearly left without me because of the hour and a half I was delayed by the Israeli authorities at the port.

It was impossible to view the lengthy search to which I was subjected as anything other than punitive, a retaliation for my refusal to answer what I considered were impudent and unnecessary questions. To anything connected with security I had responded readily enough. Yes, I had packed my luggage myself, and No, it had not been out of my hands since I had packed it, and Yes, I did understand why they were asking these questions and I was more than happy to observe their vigilance.

But as to whom I had met and talked with during my stay in Israel, I considered that to be none of their business. Had I been consorting with terrorists or plotting acts of sabotage I would hardly have admitted it to them, so the questions were in any case quite pointless. Even if many of the people who had talked to me over the past few weeks had not done so in confidence, I would still not have dreamed of naming them. But names were what was wanted, and the brash young girl who had demanded them went off to report to her superior that I was uncooperative. The outcome was a full-scale search.

They led me – a most unlikely suspect (I thought) wheeling my bright red state-of-the-art bicycle – into a small bare room. Two people stood guard behind me at the door while I was instructed to unload Roberts and place the panniers on a counter which ran down the centre between me and the chief official. Many of the books which I was directed to remove from the panniers, one by one, were studies of the various abuses of human rights in Israel over the last decades. I had been rather worried as to what their reception might be, but if the titles had any effect on the questioner I could not tell, for not a flicker of expression crossed his face as he ran an instrument over the covers and spines to detect if they concealed anything more dangerous than words.

In contrast to the orderly books was the plethora of assorted equipment that a long-distance bicyclist tends to carry – stove and cooking things, Dog Dazer for repelling fierce animals, sleeping-bag, wet weather gear (liberally covered in mud), bits of string, clothes pegs, rubber bands, candles, matches, compass, maps, tools, spare inner tubes, pens, notebooks, plastic bags, maps – and so on, and so on. Each separate item was examined and I was questioned closely on the use of the less obvious pieces. My camera had to be opened, but as I had already removed the film and sent it home this caused me no inconvenience. I was surprised not to be made to dismantle the bicycle pump – but clearly the examiner had not been told that this is the most obvious place for concealing explosives or, as I suspect, he never for a moment expected to find anything either dangerous or illegal. But both my tiny radio and the Dog Dazer had to be proved to have only innocent functions, difficult in the case of the Dog Dazer, the sound of which is inaudible to the human ear.

The attitude of the officer had started off very stiff and official, but as the interminable search proceeded it slowly changed, becoming more and more placatory. Possibly this was because I did not react to anything he did or said. I was not prepared to give him the satisfaction of letting him think I minded him going through my things, or that I was worried about the ship's imminent departure. I remained co-operative but communicated nothing more than was asked. Perhaps he became embarrassed by the pointlessness of the search, for by the finish he was making real efforts to be friendly.

The ship would in fact have sailed without me had he not possessed the authority to delay its departure. As he helped me repack the panniers and load them on to Roberts he was saying over and over again that he did not like this kind of thing; it should not be necessary, and he hoped I would forget it. I told him he had no need to apologize, but because I was tired by this time and rather fraught with the anxiety of it all I added that all police states were much the same wherever I travelled; pointless searches and questionings were not unique to Israel.

He had lingered a long time over the wide range of unusual stamps in my passport, and now, as he accompanied me down the ramp to the ship's car deck he said he would like to ask me as a traveller and a writer what I thought of Israel. I said it seemed to me that the country had got itself into a very dangerous moral predicament and that I rather doubted if it would ever be able to get out of it again. At which, with the ship hooting and the dockhands standing by to cast off the mooring ropes, he began telling me about how he had grown up in Brazil and had come to Israel because he wanted to escape corruption and live a better life, but of how hard conditions were in Israel and how he was often wondering if he had done the right thing. It was depressing, he said, to find so many countries where you could not travel on an Israeli passport.

My attention was really on trying to get aboard, but even so I was struck by the fact that like so many Jews he seemed genuinely to care about the actual ethical standing of Israel and not just the legalistic appearances. Had the ship not been on the point of departure the conversation might well have developed into another interesting exchange, with something fresh learnt on both sides. Possibly, I thought, I should see this as yet another example of Israel Shahak's small victories.

The ship was steaming out across a darkening sea long before I had secured Roberts, located my cabin and completed the boarding routine. When at last I found a place on deck from which to snatch a final glimpse of the receding coast, little could be seen except for the brilliantly lit Baha'i temple perched high above the port on the ridge of Mount Carmel. It could have been Elijah's Chariot of Fire departing heavenwards, a thought that made me realize afresh how impossibly convoluted and involved were the conflicting histories and politics of this land, not a foot of which was not deeply significant to someone.

Even during the short time I had spent in Haifa, this contentious history was again made very clear. Haifa is in Israel proper and so different to the occupied West Bank and Gaza that, as Leah Tsemel had said, it is possible to grow up there without ever seeing an Arab or of being aware that there are such things as refugee camps. I had talked with only one person while I was in Haifa, a professor of economics who had shared the same bench beside a sunny beach. I would have expected a man of his background and education to hold more reasonable views than the average in relation to the 'Palestinian Problem'. But as our conversation began to range over such issues his solution was revealed as the implacable 'Israel for Israelis' platform. 'We have nowhere else to go,' he said, reiterating the flawed and over-worked argument. 'There are twenty-seven Arab countries for them to live in. If they don't like the way things are here they should go.' And to my objection, 'But you cannot displace people who have lived in a country for two thousand years and more,' he replied: 'That's their problem, we call the shots here now.'

It was a sour note on which to leave the Holy Land, especially when added to the unpleasant exit procedure I had just been through. I felt depressed as I stood there by the rail, the ship rising and falling gently over the slight swell. One by one the stars began to stand out from the Mediterranean sky, forming themselves into the familiar patterns, and as they brightened I remembered the little village of Beit Sahour which lies so close to the Shepherds' Fields – fields named for those who once witnessed the brightest star of all coming to rest just a short way above them, over a stable on the ridge where Bethlehem stands.

In contrast to the insularity, the blatant attitude of 'might is right', I thought of Beit Sahour's role in the present struggle for the peace of the Holy Land. I thought of Simon and the other young men of the village who had spent years of their youth in Israeli prisons serving term after term of administrative detention, and who instead of letting the experience embitter them had used it to develop inner strengths. 'A chance to build a new personality, a chance to get to know yourself,' Simon had said of it. He had also claimed 'It was a privilege to be there,' and although I doubt anyone would choose a twelve month spell in an Israeli prison, it probably is a less corrupting experience than breaking the arms of your enemies' children and bulldozing their homes to the ground.

A wise Jew once said: 'The Holocaust, why do we go on so about the Holocaust? It is Germany's problem not ours.' By the same token could it not be said that the Palestinian problem ultimately affects Israel more than it does the Arabs?

The fact that Simon and his friends renounced their stone-throwing and the Molotov cocktails was not because they were afraid of the consequences, but because they grew beyond the point where they needed to answer hurt with hurt. They realized they had a choice; they could become ever more embroiled in violent reaction, which in the end would inevitably lead to out-and-out acts of terrorism, or they could find a more effective and less self-destructive form of protest.

The choice of which road to tread is made by the individual, but the strength required to oppose a repressive regime by peaceful resistance is often rooted in the faith and support of the community. This certainly was the case in Beit Sahour. Its Christian identity was its strength. It was not only the young men and boys, but everyone there who was impressive. What must it be like to see tear gas and rubber bullets used against your children; to see their limbs deliberately broken, their education continuously disrupted and their futures blighted? In Beit Sahour, as in Gaza, there were few homes free of the weight of framed photographs of imprisoned sons. That the mothers and fathers of Beit Sahour could witness such treatment of their children year after year and yet refuse to give way to hatred and bitterness was nothing short of awe-inspiring. The strength that comes from a daily battle to practise Christian forgiveness was never made clearer to me than in Beit Sahour.

What is more, it could be seen to work. Beit Sahour has proved more of a thorn in the side of the authorities than any amount of stone-throwing and sabotage. The villagers' insistence upon justice in the widely publicized stand of 'no taxation without representation' was only a beginning. In bravely bearing the consequences of that stand, in doing what they could for themselves and in resisting all attempts to break their spirit and split their ranks, they won friends for themselves even among Jewish communities.

But the real and ongoing act of subversion is Beit Sahour's insistence that a lasting peace in this troubled country requires not the separation of Jew and Palestinian, but the two communities working together to achieve peaceful co-existence and mutual understanding.

To play its part in promoting this understanding the villagers of Beit Sahour came up with the idea of inviting Israeli families to come and spend the Jewish Sabbath with them as their guests, each Jewish family to be hosted by a Palestinian Christian one. A date was fixed for the event and the village set about the preparations.

If anyone doubts the separationist policies of the Israeli administration let him explain away what followed this peaceful initiative by the villagers of Beit Sahour.

As soon as the Israeli authorities got wind of the proposed fraternization they tried to stop it. A large military presence was drafted in, the approach roads were sealed, and the area was declared a no-go military zone. To clinch matters a curfew was placed on the inhabitants of Beit Sahour. None of this, however, deterred either the Beit Sahourians or their visitors. Little-known tracks over the hills were used to bring in the Jewish families and Shabbat was duly celebrated under the unsuspecting military noses.

It was late on the following morning before the Israeli soldiers realized that Jewish and Palestinian children were playing together in the streets of Beit Sahour. After hurried consultation an officer came to order the Israelis to leave. 'We cannot,' replied the Jews. 'It is Shabbat and you know we may not travel on Shabbat.' There was little the discomforted troops could do. They could hardly employ the customary tear gas and rubber bullets against fellow Jews. Instead they ordered everyone to leave the streets and remain indoors where they would not be seen. At sunset when Shabbat ended the visitors left. But by then Jews had broken bread with Palestinians, they had also had first-hand experience of being 'on the other side' as well as a taste of the methods used by their own military against their new friends.

It was from such beginnings that the Rapprochement Centre had grown. I was able to attend only one meeting at this centre, and at the time I thought the movement too small and tenuous to be effective. In retrospect I see I was still looking for what I saw as real solutions, measurable progress, agreements at government level. I had not yet fully realized the power that even one person of good will can exercise.

There were about forty Jews and as many Palestinians

present in the Rapprochement meeting rooms. There were not chairs enough for everyone, so some sat around companionably on the ground. The Jews, both men and women, were mostly aged from around fifty to seventy with a few younger people among them. There was the air of it being something of an adventure. The Palestinians were all male, and more than half of them under thirty. The Jews had driven out to the meeting from the area of Greater Jerusalem, an area which is now effectively a huge ghetto walled by a military cordon. The Beit Sahourians like all Palestinians not registered as living in Jerusalem were of course permanently shut out of this ghetto. Perhaps it was all this that gave the meeting a flavour of the past, as though a band of citizens had ridden out secretly from a besieged medieval city to parley with the enemy.

A young Israeli sitting on the floor spoke first, staring hard at the ground and choosing his words carefully: English was the lingua franca of the meeting so it could be that he was having to think carefully about what he said and for that reason avoided any eye contact.

'I think we should start by talking about rights,' he began. 'In what sense do you recognize my right to exist?'

A Palestinian man broke in: 'This is not the time to talk about rights. We are here to talk about one state, not two. A pure Jewish state is out of the question. We have lost our land. We are here to try to co-habit.'

'Let him finish what he was saying,' directed the Palestinian chairman.

The Jewish youth continued, still gazing down at the floor. 'I think I have the right to be here. I have invested time and money in this land, and I have defended it, yes I have defended it through my time in the army.'

It was Simon who answered: 'I do not question your right to be here, but we were here maybe before you. Possibly I have Jewish blood in me too. The first Christians were Jews and my family have been here continuously since then.'

Another Palestinian took the floor. 'I do not say get rid of the Jews, only that I want my rights. I want justice and rights. I have my roots in the camps. I love my camp. I am a refugee and belong nowhere else except my camp. But still I want compensation for what has been taken from me and I want freedom to go where I want in my own land.'

'Unity,' said Simon, 'unity is what we want. No Israel, no Judah, but all of it the Holy Land. It cannot be divided. My Christian heritage makes me need not to be separated from one part of it. Part of the Middle East, yes, but not as two states, no.'

At which point the meeting split into smaller groups, one of which I joined. What struck me most forcibly about the discussions was that most of the Israelis present, intelligent though most undoubtedly were, appeared to talk from a very narrow perspective, and had little understanding of the Palestinian point of view. That they were people of goodwill I did not doubt, why else would they have been there? But the truth of what Leah Tsemel and other Jews had claimed, namely that Israel was so compartmentalized and shuttered, and that the education of the children was so slanted as to cloak the true reality of life in Israel was amply demonstrated. Which was chiefly why at the time I had seen little hope in Rapprochement's methods having any influence on peace. I thought it would take an age to get anywhere by such means.

But as the boat continued on its way northwards, out of sight of land and ever further from Jerusalem, I realized that I was missing the essential point. I had come to the Holy Land expecting to find peace, and it had been staring me in the face all the time. Everywhere I had travelled, from Cyprus, through Lebanon, Syria and Jordan, and most of all in the land that was once called Palestine, I had met people of goodwill, Muslims and Jews as well as Christians, people dedicated to peace. Like water in a dry land they were the basis for hope and new beginnings. It is not finally governments who make peace. When 'peace' has to be imposed and maintained by force it is at best an uneasy truce, as has been amply demonstrated in places like Northern Ireland and Bosnia. Real peace, King Hussein's 'a complete peace, a warm peace', when it comes, I suddenly knew with certainty, will be because there are these people, their numbers growing all the time, who will refuse to settle for anything less.

Index

Return to the Desert

A Journey from Mount Hermon to Mount Sinai

David Praill

'Man was born in the desert, in Africa. By returning to the desert he rediscovers himself ... to be lost in the desert was to find one's way to God.' *Bruce Chatwin*

In the autumn of 1993, David Praill made a journey from Mount Hermon to Mount Sinai – the length of the Holy Land. As well as raising money for the hospice of which he is manager, he was fulfilling a dream to return to the desert – for him a place of unparalleled beauty and adventure.

His forty day walk and camel ride began at a height of 8000 feet, joined the Jordan at one of its sources and descended quickly down to Galilee, and thence to Jericho. After a brief spell in Jerusalem, he walked the length of the Dead Sea and entered the Aravah desert, reaching the resort of Eilat a hundred miles later. He crossed the Sinai desert by camel with the Bedouin, arriving at St Catherine's monastery for the final ascent of Mount Sinai.

Recording the events of David Praill's journey on a daily basis, *Return to the Desert* is packed with fascinating stories about the landmarks and history of the region from Old Testament times to the political turmoil of the present day. At the same time the author, an Anglican clergyman disenchanted with the forms of his religion, discover new spiritual insight in an ancient tradition: the silence and solitude of the desert.

The American Jew

Voices from an American Jewish Community

Dan & Lavinia Cohn-Sherbok

The American Jewish community is more influential than ever before. Who are these individuals? Do they speak with one voice? How have they become so rich and powerful? What do their non-Jewish neighbours feel about them?

American rabbi Dan Cohn-Sherbok and his wife Lavinia spent four months in a typical Mid-Western city finding the answers to these questions. More than one hundred people speak for themselves, from the Orthodox rabbi to the teenage summer camper, from the self-made millionaire to the doting grand-mother, from the Auschwitz survivor to the eighteen-year-old débutante. Their stories are as gripping as the best fiction and, at the same time, provide a unique snapshot of American Jewry in the 1990s.

Dan Cohn-Sherbok teaches Jewish theology at the University of Kent, Canterbury, and is visiting Professor at Middlesex University. He is the author and editor of more than 40 books including *Holocaust Theology, The Crucified Jew, Judaism and Other Faiths* and *The Future of Judaism.*

Lavinia Cohn-Sherbok was until recently the Principal of West Heath School and is the author of *A Popular Dictionary of Judaism, A Short History of Judaism, Jewish and Christian Mysticism* and the Judaism section of *The Oxford Companion to Religion.*